First World War
and Army of Occupation
War Diary
France, Belgium and Germany

32 DIVISION
Headquarters, Branches and Services
Royal Army Ordnance Corps
Deputy Assistant Director Ordnance Services
1 April 1916 - 31 December 1918

WO95/2379/2

The Naval & Military Press Ltd
www.nmarchive.com
Published in association with The National Archives

Published by

The Naval & Military Press Ltd

Unit 10 Ridgewood Industrial Park,

Uckfield, East Sussex,

TN22 5QE England

Tel: +44 (0) 1825 749494

www.naval-military-press.com

www.nmarchive.com

This diary has been reprinted in facsimile from the original. Any imperfections are inevitably reproduced and the quality may fall short of modern type and cartographic standards.

© **Crown Copyright**
Images reproduced by permission of The National Archives, London, England, 2015.

Contents

Document type	Place/Title	Date From	Date To
Heading	WO95/2379/2		
Heading	32nd Division Divl Troops Dep. Asst Dir. Ordnance Services Apr 1916-1919 Nov.		
Heading	War Diary Of D.A.D.O.S., 32nd Division. From 1st April 1916 To 30th April 1916		
War Diary	In The Field	01/04/1916	30/04/1916
Heading	War Diary of D.A.D.O.S. 32nd Division From 1st May 1916 To 31st May 1916		
War Diary	In the field	01/05/1916	31/05/1916
Heading	War Diary of D.A.D.O.S. 32nd Division From 1st To June 30th 1916		
War Diary	In The Field	01/06/1916	30/06/1916
Heading	July 1916. War Diary of D.A.D.O.S., 32nd Division No 4 Volume 1		
War Diary	In The Field	01/07/1916	31/07/1916
Heading	War Diary Of D.A.D.O.S., 32nd Division. For August 1916. No 5 Volume 1		
War Diary	In The Field	01/08/1916	31/08/1916
Heading	War Diary Of D.A.D.O.S., 32nd Division. No 6 Volume 1		
War Diary	In The Field	01/09/1916	30/09/1916
Miscellaneous	D.A.D.O.S., 32nd Division.	01/10/1916	01/10/1916
Heading	War Diary Of D.A.D.O.S., 32 Division. Volume 1 No. 7		
War Diary	In The Field	01/10/1916	31/10/1916
Heading	War Diary Of D.A.D.O.S., 32nd Division. Volume 1 No. 8		
War Diary	In The Field	01/11/1916	30/11/1916
War Diary	December 1916 War Diary of D.A.O.G.S. 32nd Division. No 9 Volume 1		
War Diary	In The Field	01/12/1916	21/12/1916
Heading	January 1917. War Diary of D.A.O.G.S. 32nd Division. No Volume 2		
War Diary	In The Field	01/01/1917	31/01/1917
Heading	War Diary Of D.A.D.O.S., 32nd Division. Volume 2 No 2		
War Diary	In The Field	01/02/1917	28/02/1917
Heading	War Diary Of D.A.D.O.S., 32nd Division. Volume 2 No 3		
War Diary	In The Field	01/03/1917	31/03/1917
Heading	War Diary Of D.A.D.O.S. 32 Division. Volume 2 No. 4		
War Diary	In The Field	01/04/1917	22/04/1917
Heading	War Diary Of D.A.D.O.S., 32 Division. Volume 2 No 5		
War Diary	In The Field	04/05/1917	31/05/1917
Heading	War Diary Of D.A.D.O.S., 32 Division. Volume 2 No-6		
War Diary	In The Field	01/06/1917	30/06/1917
Heading	War Diary Of D.A.D.O.S. 32nd Divn Volume 2 No-4		

War Diary	In The Field	01/07/1917	31/07/1917
Heading	War Diary Of D A D O S 32nd Division. Volume. 2 No 8		
War Diary	In The Field	01/08/1917	31/08/1917
Heading	War Diary Of D.A.D.O.S. 32nd Divn. Volume 2 No-9		
War Diary	In The Field	01/09/1917	30/09/1917
Heading	War Diary Of D.A.D.O.S., 32 Divn. For October 1917 Vol 19		
War Diary	In The Field	01/10/1917	31/10/1917
War Diary	In The Field	01/11/1917	30/11/1917
Heading	War Diary For The Month Of December 1917 D.A.D.O.S., 32nd Division. Vol 21		
War Diary	In The Field	01/12/1917	31/12/1917
War Diary	In The Field	01/01/1918	31/01/1918
Heading	War Diary Of D.A.D.O.S. 32nd Division. Vol 23		
War Diary	In The Field	01/02/1918	28/02/1918
War Diary	In The Field	01/03/1918	31/03/1918
War Diary	In The Field	01/04/1918	30/04/1918
War Diary	In The Field	01/05/1918	31/05/1918
War Diary	In The Field	01/06/1918	30/06/1918
Heading	War Diary of D.A.D.O.S, 32nd Division Vol 3-No. 7 (July 1918)		
War Diary	In The Field	01/07/1918	31/07/1918
Heading	War Diary Of 1 D.A.D.O.S, 32nd (Brit) Division. Vol.3-No. 8 August 1918		
War Diary	In The Field	01/08/1918	31/08/1918
Heading	War Diary Of D.A.D.O.S. 32nd (Brit) Division. Vol. 3 No 9		
War Diary	In The Field	01/09/1918	30/09/1918
Heading	War Diary Of D.A.D.O.S. 32nd (Brit) Div. Vol 3-No 10		
War Diary	In The Field	01/10/1918	31/10/1918
Heading	War Diary Of D.A.D.O.S. 32nd (Brit) Division Vol.3		
War Diary	In The Field	01/11/1918	30/11/1918
Heading	War Diary Of D.A.D.O.S. 32nd Div. December 1918 Vol. 3-No. 12		
War Diary	In The Field	01/12/1918	31/12/1918

WO 97/23379 (2)

32ND DIVISION
DIVL TROOPS

DEP. ASST DIR. ORDNANCE SERVICES

APR 1916 - ~~DEC 1918~~
1917 NOV

32ND DIVISION
DIVL TROOPS

DADOS 32 Div Vol 1

Confidential

War Diary
of
D. A. D. O. S.
32nd Division

From 1st April 1916 to 30th April 1916

Dec 18

Army Form C. 2118.

WAR DIARY
or
INTELLIGENCE SUMMARY.
(Erase heading not required.)

Instructions regarding War Diaries and Intelligence Summaries are contained in F. S. Regs., Part II. and the Staff Manual respectively. Title pages will be prepared in manuscript.

Place	Date	Hour	Summary of Events and Information	Remarks and references to Appendices
In the Field.	1/4/16		Nothing out of the ordinary routine to report.	
	2/4/16		26 Lewis machine guns received from Base. This completes the 13 Batt'ns to 8 per Batt'n. Also received the full consignment of P.H. Anti Gas Helmets to complete the Division to the second P.H. Helmet per Officer & man. Moved the Dump from Henencourt to Senlis after long issue of same.	
	3/4/16		Held the fortnightly conference of Quartermasters with the support of the D.A.Q.M.G. who kindly makes a point of attending to back me up owing to my junior rank. Several points of difficulty in regard to indenting cleared up. I find these conferences very helpful. Two of the Trail Staff Captains also attended. Received 15 bicycles to issue to Interpreters in lieu of Horses.	
	4/4/16.		Visited the divisional Shoemakers, Armourer, Tailors & Forge shops under my charge & found all in full work which was satisfactory as they had only moved down from their Chateau the previous evening.	

T.J134. Wt. W708—776. 500000. 4/15. Sir J. C. & S.

Army Form C. 2118.

WAR DIARY
or
INTELLIGENCE SUMMARY.
(Erase heading not required.)

Instructions regarding War Diaries and Intelligence Summaries are contained in F. S. Regs., Part II. and the Staff Manual respectively. Title pages will be prepared in manuscript.

Place	Date	Hour	Summary of Events and Information	Remarks and references to Appendices
In the Field.	5/4/16.		Proceeded to Railhead & Amiens to local purchase of an unimportant nature. Ordinary Routine work.	
	6/4/16.		Issued 20 Harp shaped Perisopes to the Brigade in the line the trench stores by favourable reports received on them. Arranged a Brigade dump at Contay for Brigade in the Back area now Construction of Trench Lamp to be sent shortly to be at Contay at 10 a.m.	
	7/4/16.		Nothing to report.	
	8/4/16.		Proceeded to Amiens to see some female carriers under instructions from the G.O.C. to make other local purchases. Nothing to report in the rest of the day.	
	9/4/16.		Proceeded to Railhead to arrange with R.O.O. for return of winter clothing	

Army Form C. 2118.

WAR DIARY
or
INTELLIGENCE SUMMARY.
(Erase heading not required.)

Instructions regarding War Diaries and Intelligence Summaries are contained in F. S. Regs., Part II. and the Staff Manual respectively. Title pages will be prepared in manuscript.

Place	Date	Hour	Summary of Events and Information	Remarks and references to Appendices
In the Field	10/4/16.		Held a conference of Quartermasters received instructions as to the return of winter clothing. Went in Back Area to bring three things to a Point arranged at Cateny under charge of B.Q.D. The remainder to being E.H.Q. Group.	
	11/4/16.		Demanded 20,000 P.H. Helmets from Base as Divisional Reserve. Received 7 lamps electric Signalling out of 22 demanded to replace Lamps Liege (candle) & issued them.	
	12/4/16.		Accepted undercoats fur & leather jerkins from units that are moving forward than transport. Several damaged steel helmets returned from casualties. In some cases they have undoubtedly saved the life of the wearer. Armoury Routine.	
	13/4/16.		Demanded 38 revised Sprayers to replace others left behind in taking up fresh positions, to help complete to Divisional scale of 100.	

T.131. Wt. W708-776. 500000. 4/15. Sir J. C. & S.

WAR DIARY
or
INTELLIGENCE SUMMARY.

(Erase heading not required.)

Army Form C. 2118.

Instructions regarding War Diaries and Intelligence Summaries are contained in F. S. Regs., Part II. and the Staff Manual respectively. Title pages will be prepared in manuscript.

Place	Date	Hour	Summary of Events and Information	Remarks and references to Appendices
In the Field.	14/4/16.		Received 25 Dayfield pattern shields for protection of Bomb Throwers to be issued on trial. 20 were issued to 97 Brigade to put on report. Proceeded to Amiens for Local Purchases.	
	15/4/16.		Busy all day receiving returned Winter Clothing. Nothing out of the ordinary to report.	
	16/4/16.		Proceeded to Railhead + X Corps H.Q. to arrange as to what articles should be sent next day as I have to have much with X Corps. Arranged Revd Blankets. Returned via Contay to see how the return of Winter Clothing was proceeding at Group there.	
	17/4/16.		Despatched 1446 Blankets to Railhead & went myself to see them loaded. Nothing further to report.	
	18/4/16.		Demanded 16 Vickers machine Guns from Base to replace 16 Maxims in possession of the 1st Bde Machine Gun Coy. Board of survey held on Returned Winter Clothing	

WAR DIARY
or
INTELLIGENCE SUMMARY.

(Erase heading not required.)

Army Form C. 2118.

Place	Date	Hour	Summary of Events and Information	Remarks and references to Appendices
In the Field	19/4/16		Despatched 1295 Blankets to Paris in continuation of Return of winter clothing, & sent to Railhead & then on to Rouen for local Purchase.	
	20/4/16		Ordinary Routine work. Despatched 2620 Blankets to Paris.	
	21/4/16		Despatched 600 Blankets to Paris. Received 1 Telescope Jarrum. One of two to be issued in lieu of lighter pattern under manufacture. Received & issued 16 Kitchen Suits to the Sup. Col.	
	22/4/16		Despatched 190 Coats Sheepskin lined and 1820 Undercoats fur to Paris. Went to Railhead myself & arrange for next days despatch.	
	23/4/16		Despatched 3630 Jerkins Leather. Ordinary Routine work.	
	24/4/16		Had a whole truck allotted & despatched 160 Coats Sheepskin lined, 775 Undercoats Fur and 2850 Jerkins Leather. Attended Railhead & had another whole Truck allotted for 27th.	

Army Form C. 2118.

WAR DIARY
or
INTELLIGENCE SUMMARY.
(Erase heading not required.)

Instructions regarding War Diaries and Intelligence Summaries are contained in F.S. Regs., Part II. and the Staff Manual respectively. Title pages will be prepared in manuscript.

Place	Date	Hour	Summary of Events and Information	Remarks and references to Appendices
In the Field	25/4/16.		Received 8 shell jackets for Trench Mortar Batteries. To settle where an extra shell jacket put on back & front so that 6 shells can be carried in place of 4. Went to Amiens for local Purchases.	
	26/4/16.		Held Fortnightly conference of Quartermasters. The Question of Head Ropes was discussed. Very heavy wastage owing to Horses eating the Ropes & Reins. Brattice hide. D.A.D.V.S. asked to bring forward the suggestion that Chain Collar be issued for horses. Minor difficulties cleared up.	
	27/4/16.		Despatched 160 Cords Sheepskin lined. 1410 undercoats Fur and 1900 leather jerkins to Paris. Attended Railhead.	
	28/4/16.		Shared Truck with I Corps Troops & despatched 640 Rugs Horse & was allotted whole Truck for next day.	
	29/4/16.		Despatched 1970 Blankets. Nothing further to report. From Center 850 / 2620	

WAR DIARY
or
INTELLIGENCE SUMMARY.
(Erase heading not required.)

Army Form C. 2118.

Place	Date	Hour	Summary of Events and Information	Remarks and references to Appendices
In the Field	30/4/16		The following work has been turned out of Divisional shops under my charge for this month.	
			Tailors shop. 3 men	
			Shoemakers shop. 7 men	*Only 2 of these men are experts. The others are learning. 7 att.
			Forge * 12 men	
			Bags Nose repaired 394. Cmt Buckets 95. Hays for tactical purpose 389. Cord sleeve ropes No. 12	Boots repaired 1341/m 456 fm shoes Horse
			The Fortnightly Conference of Quartermasters has had a good effect as indents are more regularly submitted + also rendered in more correct form + this has lightened the work of this office + saved delay in forwarding indents to the Base.	

F.M.Urquhart Lieut.
D.A.D.O.S. 32 Div

DADOS 32D Vol 2

<u>Confidential</u>

War Diary of

D.A.D.O.S.

32nd Division.

from 1st May 1916
to
31st May 1916.

Army Form C. 2118.

WAR DIARY
or
INTELLIGENCE SUMMARY.
(Erase heading not required.)

Instructions regarding War Diaries and Intelligence Summaries are contained in F. S. Regs., Part II. and the Staff Manual respectively. Title pages will be prepared in manuscript.

Place	Date	Hour	Summary of Events and Information	Remarks and references to Appendices
In Field.	1/5/16		Attended Railhead made arrangements with R.O.O. as to class of returned trouser clothing to be boiled in truck next day or Reported to Paris. Ordinary Routine work for the rest of the day.	
	2/5/16		Despatched 197 bundles of ten each of Blankets to yesterday. Proceeded to Amiens to bring out 25 Lewis Mach. Gun covers & 153 grenade waistcoats purchased locally under authority of G.O.C. Found a sample of boot with leather top for issue to each battalion for Trench Guard, the price of Nubk Boots as complaints were made that men fingers gor frostbites pulling out the runs. These were made in several Trenches shops from any strip of leather & the hooks for supporting bolt from serviceable S.B. Jackets.	
	3/5/16		Proceeded to Amiens to purchase 12 Electric Torches under authority of G.O.C for a Special enterprise. Nothing out of ordinary routine during the rest of the day.	

WAR DIARY
or
INTELLIGENCE SUMMARY

Army Form C. 2118.

Place	Date	Hour	Summary of Events and Information	Remarks and references to Appendices
In the Field.	4/5/16		Visited 13.A.C. 153rd Brigade on matters of spare gun parts. Indent not necessary. Also found a lot of surplus harness ordered its return to Ordnance. In the afternoon visited Batteries C-164 and C-161 in the line. Everything satisfactory & no complaints from them as to Ordnance supplies. Impressed upon them the correct procedure when guns are damaged or are out of action from lack of small spare parts or more serious damages.	
	5/5/16.		Despatched 14/18 pdr G.F.S. Boots to Paris. No truck up from Base with stores. Proceeded to Amiens for urgent local purchases of paint required for flags for tactical manoeuvres. Routine work.	
	6/5/16.		Nothing to report.	
	7/5/16.		Despatched G.S.O. for of gun Boots through to Base. Two lorries at Poulchard as Trucks had miscarried. Sent two lorries to Heavy Motor Workshop to get 15 hand carts for T.M. Battys of this Division. Practice fire alarms supplied 100 Trench mortar cases. Noted workshop tree that all were alert.	

T.134. Wt. W708—776. 500000. 4/15. Sir J. C. & S.

Army Form C. 2118.

WAR DIARY
or
INTELLIGENCE SUMMARY.
(Erase heading not required.)

Instructions regarding War Diaries and Intelligence Summaries are contained in F. S. Regs., Part II. and the Staff Manual respectively. Title pages will be prepared in manuscript.

Place	Date	Hour	Summary of Events and Information	Remarks and references to Appendices
In the Field.	8/5/16		Held fortnightly conference of Quarter Masters & dealt with several points. S.A.O.M.S. made to attend. Proceeded to Amiens for urgent purchase of white calico re. Flags for tactical manoeuvres. Despatched 1690 blankets to Rhins. visited the Shops.	
	9/5/16		Nothing to report.	
	10/5/16		Received 55 trees for carrying down magazines & 1000 magazines. Also 25 harp shaped Periscopes. Proceeded to Amiens for urgent local Purchase.	
	11/5/16		Proceeded to Railhead to oversee the despatch of 2160 fishermen leather 35 coats sheepskin & 200 undercoats, fur. arranged to further the despatch of small lot for next day. Called on A.D.O.S. & Capt. & see if he had any instructions to give. Nothing of any urgency. Nothing further to report.	
	12/5/16		Proceeded to X Corps to hand over a German trophy to A.D.O.S. This was a tin box with holes for 3 contact plugs & was filled with an explosive. Size of box slightly larger than a 100 cigarette box.	

T.134. Wt. W708—776. 500000. 4/16. Sir J. C. & S.

Army Form C. 2118.

WAR DIARY
or
INTELLIGENCE SUMMARY.
(Erase heading not required.)

Instructions regarding War Diaries and Intelligence Summaries are contained in F.S. Regs., Part II. and the Staff Manual respectively. Title pages will be prepared in manuscript.

Place	Date	Hour	Summary of Events and Information	Remarks and references to Appendices
In the field	12/5/16		This was captured in German trench near Thiepval on 9/5/16. Probably a detonator for mine. Went on to Railhead. Visited by S.T.O.O.I. of 8th Division to see the shops under my charge as he has been ordered to start them in his Division. Also visited by S.O.O.S. 4th Army.	
	13/5/16		The D.D.O.S. X Corps came this morning + inspected the Dumps + went thro' incomplete indents + visited the shops. Nothing out of the ordinary routine to report.	
	14/5/16		Held Board of Survey on Returned Motor Clothing + Horse Rugs. Board composed of Major Stage + Capt Stone 13th Lancs Fus. + Lieut Urquhart (Gordons) whole day taken up with the work.	
	15/5/16		Proceeded to Railhead + 8th Corps H.Q. on took over a burnt out German incendiary bomb dropped from an aeroplane in the vicinity. Despatched two Truckloads of Rugs House to Paris.	

WAR DIARY or INTELLIGENCE SUMMARY.

Army Form C. 2118.

(Erase heading not required.)

Place	Date	Hour	Summary of Events and Information	Remarks and references to Appendices
In the field	16/5/16		Visited by A.D.O.S. I Corps. Brought to his notice defective magazines for Lewis machine guns sent up in last consignment from base. The Unit reported 42 defective out of 80 another 80 out of 127 these tried second to reports from Units sent in to A.D.O.S. point out all reports not in. Large number reported defective. A.D.O.S. took the defective magazines to 4th Army. Went to D.A.C. in the afternoon to clear up the matter of reorganization of D.A.C. & pushed absorption of B.A.C.	
	17/5/16		Visited 14 F.A. "Bde H.Qr. to hasten reply of defective magazines, all reports not yet in. Went to Raincheval in the afternoon to inform R.O.O. that I had no returned clothing to return tomorrow. Arranged for truck to go to 21st Div. Gun Book Thiepval. Proceeded to Amiens for local purchase. A.D.O.S. I Corps came during my absence. Armourer acting magazines Lewis M.G.)	
	18/5/16		day not all in yet.	

Army Form C. 2118.

WAR DIARY
or
INTELLIGENCE SUMMARY.
(Erase heading not required.)

Instructions regarding War Diaries and Intelligence Summaries are contained in F. S. Regs., Part II. and the Staff Manual respectively. Title pages will be prepared in manuscript.

Place	Date	Hour	Summary of Events and Information	Remarks and references to Appendices
In the Field	19/5/16		Received one Lewis machine Gun & replace one damaged by shell fire to 15th H.L.I. Drew 25 Steel helmets with improvements for issue 14 printed Khaki Drill Clowns & 11 Green from O.O. 4th Army Troops & 144 Receipts & handed the latter to I Corps for distribution	
	20/5/16		Nothing to Report.	
	21/5/16		Proceeded to Pont Noyelle to take Gas School & then to see A.D.O.S X Corps where some stores from O.A. I Corps on Railhead & DADOS 36th Div & HQ 97 Inf Bde to deliver urgent were picked up on this round.	
	22/5/16		Ordinary Routine work.	
	23/5/16		Went to Querrieu to get 2 Mountee Horses from OD 4th Army Troops. Demanded 23 Mountee Horses & 81 Cylinders complete to new scale of 35 Horses & 105 Cylinders per Division.	

T.134. Wt. W708-776. 500000. 4/15. Sir J. C. & S.

Army Form C. 2118.

WAR DIARY
or
INTELLIGENCE SUMMARY.
(Erase heading not required.)

Instructions regarding War Diaries and Intelligence Summaries are contained in F. S. Regs., Part II. and the Staff Manual respectively. Title pages will be prepared in manuscript.

Place	Date	Hour	Summary of Events and Information	Remarks and references to Appendices
In the Field	24/5/16.		Visited by A.D.S. I Corps who made an inspection of transport. No faults found. Proceeded to Amiens for local purchase of urgent stores.	
	25/5/16.		Nothing to report.	
	26/5/16.		Had seven horse shoes/experiences returned from front line with broken miners. According to report from there these shattered by concussion of gun fire, not by direct hits. Perhaps better shoes could be used in these circumstances as these might be fitted with indiarubber.	
	27/5/16.		Proceeded to I Corps H.Qrs. A.D.S. reports the recent delay in arrival of trucks. The last month he being short much left stores on Thursday did not arrive at Railhead till Saturday afternoon when the goods are closed for the day & the stores are not available till Sunday. Sent written report on the matter.	

Army Form C. 2118.

WAR DIARY
or
INTELLIGENCE SUMMARY.
(Erase heading not required.)

Instructions regarding War Diaries and Intelligence Summaries are contained in F. S. Regs., Part II. and the Staff Manual respectively. Title pages will be prepared in manuscript.

Place	Date	Hour	Summary of Events and Information	Remarks and references to Appendices
In the field.	28/5/16.		Made an inspection of Quarter master Stores of three units as ordered by G.O.C. Free if there was any accumulation of stores. These three units were quite satisfactory in this respect. Received encouragement if men were careless in attaching tripe which complete the Services. Would note if by per Bn??	
	29/5/16.		Proceeded to Railhead & was informed there that the Railhead would be moved to Achiene on the next day 30E. Returned Stores can only be accepted two days a week as only two wagons are at present there & full trucks have to sent. This does not of course apply to the Winter Clothing.	
	30/5/16.		Visited by A.D.V.S. X Corps with reference to more complete records being kept. Inspected all our books & found that a complete record was kept. That we could comply with the suggested scheme at once. Later Proceeded to Amien for bread purchase & inspected 2 more 2 M Store. on the way. Both satisfactory.	

Army Form C. 2118.

WAR DIARY
or
INTELLIGENCE SUMMARY.
(Erase heading not required.)

Place	Date	Hour	Summary of Events and Information	Remarks and references to Appendices
In the field	31/5/16		Superintended securing of the second Flusher for men. Received orders from XVIIth Corps to send 5000 of these to the Casualty Clearing Station in the Pack weather convenient. Received 234 special O.H.G. helmets with elastic outside. The following work has been done in the shops under my charge during this month.	

Forge.
Shoes those for 440.
Cradle sketches 26.

Tailors shop.
Miscellaneous 516.
Flags 575.
Trench helmet covers 80.
Shell jackets altered 52.
" " new 31

Shoemakers Shop.
Boots repaired 1363 /pa.

Wilgrehost Capt.
D.A.D.O.S.
32 Div.

DADOS 32 Div Vol 3

Confidential

War Diary

of

D A D O S

32nd Division

June 1st to June 30th 1916

Army Form C. 2118.

WAR DIARY
or
INTELLIGENCE SUMMARY.
(Erase heading not required.)

Instructions regarding War Diaries and Intelligence Summaries are contained in F. S. Regs., Part II. and the Staff Manual respectively. Title pages will be prepared in manuscript.

Place	Date	Hour	Summary of Events and Information	Remarks and references to Appendices
In the field	1/6/16		Held a Board of Survey on Second Howitzer + reports. Also a conference of Quartermasters. Completed figures of Bulk issues despatched. War Diary + Supplest accounts for May.	
	2/6/16		Proceeded on leave of absence.	
	11/6/16		Returned from Leave.	
	12/6/16		Proceeded to Railhead + X Corps Headquarters & saw A.D.O.S.	
			Nothing out of ordinary routine to report.	
	13/6/16		Wired to Base to send 2 in Trench Mortar for Z 32 to replace one damaged by shell fire. Ordinary routine work.	
	14/6/16		Wired to Base for O.D.F. 18 ph fuse only for B 168 condemned by I.O.M. for shooting short.	
	15/6/16		Daylight-saving Bill came into force. Clock an hour deep. 20 French Batts signalling lamps came up to issue viveres issued as follows. C.R.A. 5. Inf Bde. 40 Qn 1 each + 1 per Battn.	

Army Form C. 2118.

WAR DIARY
or
INTELLIGENCE SUMMARY.
(Erase heading not required.)

Instructions regarding War Diaries and Intelligence Summaries are contained in F.S. Regs., Part II. and the Staff Manual respectively. Title pages will be prepared in manuscript.

Place	Date	Hour	Summary of Events and Information	Remarks and references to Appendices
In the Field.	16/6/16.		Received the 2 - T.M. for Z 32 & issued it same day. Proceeded to Amiens for Coal Purchase.	
	17/6/16.		Proceeded to Puchevillers & 10th Corps to take part in a conference of D.A.D.O.S. of 10th Corps with A.D.O.S. who gave us our instructions in regard to the active operations about to take place. He gave us a large measure of freedom as to the disposal of our Staffs. O.F.7. 18/o for B. 168 came up & were delivered to Battery.	
	18/6/16.		Worked out scheme in consultation with the Chief Clerk & went to Railhead to arrange with R.T.O. as to times of Unloading Trucks. Visited S.S.O. to arrange for stores to be drawn at the Refilling Point of Division. Arranged with O.C. Sail Train to attach W.D. Detainments to the Company of the Train.	
	19/6/16		Had to alter all arrangements made owing to huns shelling Fienvy altered which made it impossible to use stores.	

T/134. Wt. W708-776. 500000. 4/15. Sir J.C. & S.

Army Form C. 2118.

WAR DIARY
or
INTELLIGENCE SUMMARY.
(Erase heading not required.)

Place	Date	Hour	Summary of Events and Information	Remarks and references to Appendices
In the Field	19/6/16.		received from Railhead the Tuesday.	
	20/6/16.		Sent out the Bde W.O.'s & their storemen & Repelling Point spreads each with a tent Tarpaulin. Each Bn's clerk is to stay with the lorry & be attached to supply Column. By this means I have an automatic connection between Railhead & Repelling point. The clerk with the lorry proceeds direct to Railhead where I meet him. The stores are distributed to the different Brigade lorries by myself & are then taken to Repelling point & dumped ready to come the following morning by B.G.O.	
	21/6/16.		Proceeded to Railhead & distributed stores from truck. It took an hour & a half, & we were clean by specified time. Went on to Repelling point & saw that all was in order.	

WAR DIARY
or
INTELLIGENCE SUMMARY.
(Erase heading not required.)

Army Form C. 2118.

Place	Date	Hour	Summary of Events and Information	Remarks and references to Appendices
In the Field	22/6/16		Proceeded to Railhead & distributed from Truck. Things worked better & had finished in an hour. Proceeded to Papillory Wait & on to Amiens for urgent stores Purchase.	
	23/6/16		Had to be at Railhead at 6 a.m. as hours are changed. Work went well & were away before 8 a.m. Proceeded to Amiens to Purchase safety pins for fireing gas Helmets - no troops or emergency rations. 250 pars purchased.	
	24/6/16		Railhead & ordinary routine work.	
	25/6/16		Railhead duties. Sent to Beauval for 2 2" Trench Mortars. Ordinary Routine work.	
	26/6/16		Railhead duties. 5 T.M. Reb. arrived & one 240 m.m. T.M. from Base.	

Army Form C. 2118.

WAR DIARY
or
INTELLIGENCE SUMMARY.
(Erase heading not required.)

Instructions regarding War Diaries and Intelligence Summaries are contained in F. S. Regs., Part II. and the Staff Manual respectively. Title pages will be prepared in manuscript.

Place	Date	Hour	Summary of Events and Information	Remarks and references to Appendices
In the Field.	27/6/16		Railhead Station. System working well. Proceeded to Struein to purchase 1½" rope urgently required. I Corps H.Q. moved at Beulu.	
	28/6/16		Ordinary Routine work.	
	29/6/16		Moved to Base for O.R.F. 18 pr. for A. 164 discharged to shell fire. also for one Lewis Gun for 16 Lancs.	
	30/6/16		Ordinary Routine work. Lewis Gun arrived at Railhead at 4 p.m. Fetched it in car & delivered it personally to unit in Front line. 18 pr. gun also notified for the following morning.	

Wilson Lechoiret Capt.
D A O T S 32 Div

1/7/16

Confidential.

July 1916

War Diary of
D.A.D.O.S.
32nd Division

No 4

Volume 1

Army Form C. 2118.

WAR DIARY
or
INTELLIGENCE SUMMARY.
(Erase heading not required.)

Instructions regarding War Diaries and Intelligence Summaries are contained in F. S. Regs., Part II. and the Staff Manual respectively. Title pages will be prepared in manuscript.

Place	Date	Hour	Summary of Events and Information	Remarks and references to Appendices
In the Field.	1/7/16		The Great Offensive began at 7-30. Attended Railhead at 5 am. & distributed stores as usual. Received one 18 pr for A.164 with carriage but without Breech mechanism.	
	2/7/16		Railhead as usual. Ordinary Routine work.	
	3/7/16		Ordinary Routine work. Received one 4.5" howitzer for D.161, & 2 dial sights no 7 for C.164 & handed dial sight no 26" to L.O. one X Corps.	
	4/7/16		Division withdrawn from Battle & H.Q. removed to Contay. Received & issued one Vickers gun & to 14 Bde Mach. Gun Coy. & one 18 pr for A.164.	
	5/7/16		Received one Stokes mortar for 14" Bde T.M. Batty. issued same.	
	6/7/16		Division ordered forward again. H.Q. return to Senlis. Ordinary routine work.	
	7/7/16		Moved back to Senlis. Ordinary routine work.	

Army Form C. 2118.

WAR DIARY
or
INTELLIGENCE SUMMARY.
(Erase heading not required.)

Place	Date	Hour	Summary of Events and Information	Remarks and references to Appendices
In the Field	8/7/16		Ordinary Routine work	
	9/7/16		Ordinary Routine work. G.O.C. Divnl Artillery called personally to thank us for the way the guns had been kept in action & the rapidity with which Guns & Spare parts came up. Explained that it was due to the splendid organisation at Base. Went the only time or second that anyone has been aware that Ordnance Dept. existed.	
	10/7/16		Received 2 Vickers guns for 97" Bde Mach. Gun Coy. & 1 for 96" Bde Mach Gun Coy. Also 6 Lewis guns for 1st Dorsets + 2 for 17" H.L.I. also one from 49" Divn for 2" K.O.Y.L.I.	
	11/7/16		Received one 4-5 how for D.155. Also 4 Lewis guns for 11 "Borders, & 4 for 16" K.O.Y.L.I. and 3 for the 16" N.F. also one Lewis from 49" Divn for 16" Lancs Fus. also one Vickers for 96" Bde Mach Gun Coy. Also 2 rifle Breech mechanism for X.32 T.M.B.	

Army Form C. 2118.

WAR DIARY
or
INTELLIGENCE SUMMARY.
(Erase heading not required.)

Instructions regarding War Diaries and Intelligence Summaries are contained in F. S. Regs., Part II. and the Staff Manual respectively. Title pages will be prepared in manuscript.

Place	Date	Hour	Summary of Events and Information	Remarks and references to Appendices
In the Field	12/7/16		Received 5 Stokes mortar 3 inch for 97" Bde T.M. Batty also 4 Stokes mortar 3 inch for 14" Bde T.M. Batty.	
	13/7/16		H.Q. Division moved to Bouzincourt. Ordinary Routine work.	
	14/7/16		Ordinary Routine work.	
	15/7/16		Ordinary Routine work.	
	16/7/16		Division withdrawn from the line. H.Q. moved to Beauval. Handed over Store tent to A.D.O.S. 48" Divn + removed all stores to Beauval.	
	17/7/16		Divn H.Q. moved to Doullens. Carried all stores forward.	
	18/7/16		Remained in Doullens.	

T.2134. Wt. W708-776. 500000. 4/15. Sir J.C. & S.

Army Form C. 2118.

WAR DIARY
or
INTELLIGENCE SUMMARY.
(Erase heading not required.)

Instructions regarding War Diaries and Intelligence Summaries are contained in F. S. Regs., Part II. and the Staff Manual respectively. Title pages will be prepared in manuscript.

Place	Date	Hour	Summary of Events and Information	Remarks and references to Appendices
In the Field	19/7/16		Received A.D.Q. moved to Flers. Distributed 600 pairs socks to 96" Inf. Bde. on the march. Sent all my stores to Bryas to meet me there.	
	20/7/16		Div. H.Q. moved to Bryas. Distributed a further 1200 pairs socks to 96" Inf Bde. on the march.	
	21/7/16		Loaded all shops stuff on train at St Pol to be forwarded to own destination as lorries were getting overworked with making 2 trips each march to keep all the stuff together. Moved the Balance to Dillers. Went on to Dillers to arrange for billets for Divnl. workshops. Found good place.	
	22/7/16		5 Truck loads of Stores at Railhead. Very busy issuing & hastening re-equipment of Division.	
	23/7/16		3 more trucks arrived. Good deal issued during the day.	

Army Form C. 2118.

WAR DIARY
or
INTELLIGENCE SUMMARY.
(Erase heading not required.)

Instructions regarding War Diaries and Intelligence Summaries are contained in F. S. Regs., Part II. and the Staff Manual respectively. Title pages will be prepared in manuscript.

Place	Date	Hour	Summary of Events and Information	Remarks and references to Appendices
Lillers	24/7/16		Ordinary routine work.	
	25/7/16		Divisional HQ to move to Bethune tomorrow. Got the Dump pretty well clear + ordered the shops to get packed up ready to move in the morning. Visits by ADOS, 1st Corps.	
	26/7/16		Arrived at Bethune 9 a.m. Found no billets allotted for shops. Had great difficulty in finding suitable places. Succeeded after 4 hrs search.	
	27/7/16		Started shops going again + got the Dump in order. All miscellaneous stores sorted out - + can now carry on in some sort of good order as we seem likely to stay here at least a week.	
	28/7/16		Stores coming up very well + equipment progressing well. First unit extemporised with clothing + boots. MG technical stores now due.	

Army Form C. 2118.

WAR DIARY
or
INTELLIGENCE SUMMARY.
(Erase heading not required.)

Instructions regarding War Diaries and Intelligence Summaries are contained in F. S. Regs., Part II. and the Staff Manual respectively. Title pages will be prepared in manuscript.

Place	Date	Hour	Summary of Events and Information	Remarks and references to Appendices
In the Field	29/7/16		Received 16,400 P.H.G. Anstle helmets to complete division 6 over for officers + men. Ordinary Routine work.	
	30/7/16		Ordinary routine work.	
	31/7/16		Visited by A.D.O.S. 1st Corps + Inspector of Armourers also spent some time in Shop in getting out scheme for running these shops on their own lines.	

W Urquhart Capt
D.A.D.O.S.

1/8/16

Vol 5

Confidential

War Diary

of

D.A.D.O.S.

32nd Division

for

August 1916.

N° 5

Volume 1

WAR DIARY or INTELLIGENCE SUMMARY

Army Form C. 2118

(Erase heading not required.)

Place	Date	Hour	Summary of Events and Information	Remarks and references to Appendices
In the Field	1/8/16.		Ordinary Routine Work.	
	2/8/16.		Ordinary Routine work.	
	3/8/16.		Inspector of Armourers arrived to inspect the Armr Shop. He seemed satisfied after spending some time in the Shops.	
	4/8/16.		Took Inspector of Armourers to Sniping School & inspected the A.D.O.S. I Corps.	
	5/8/16.		Took Inspector of Armourers to 8" Divn. Ordinary routine work. Stores coming up very well.	
	6/8/16.		Attended Church Parade held by Army Commander Commencement 2nd year of war.	
	7/8/16.		Held Quarter masters conference at 11am to replenish many of the regulations issued by 1st Corps in regard to Ordnance Stores. Town shelled with 15" shells by Bosche beginning at 12-15 p.m. Shelling lasted for 1¾ hrs. Went with Inspector of Armourers to	

WAR DIARY
or
INTELLIGENCE SUMMARY
(Erase heading not required.)

Army Form C. 2118

Place	Date	Hour	Summary of Events and Information	Remarks and references to Appendices
In the field	7/8/16		Saarbruck & St Ouen to try & purchase steel spring wire to repair defective springs in Lewis Gun Magazines. Went at 2-30 after shelling had ceased	
	8/8/16		Spent most of the day looking for new offices as our proper one as another Div. is moving into Bethune. Found suitable place but rather poor place for the Group.	
	9/8/16		Shelled again with rather stuff probably 5-9". Doing office work under the circumstances rather difficult.	
	10/8/16		Moved into new premises. Sighted corps of Army Ordnance as storeroom & office restore. A few more shells. Not a healthy spot.	
	11/8/16		More shells. One about 50 yds up the street. Ordnance Portable took.	
	12/8/16		Shells fell near the Group, & Armourers Shop which by payment. No casualties, but work rather disorganised for the afternoon.	

WAR DIARY
or
INTELLIGENCE SUMMARY
(Erase heading not required.)

Army Form C. 2118

Place	Date	Hour	Summary of Events and Information	Remarks and references to Appendices
In the Field	13/9/16		Carried out inspection of vehicles of 96" & 97" Infantry Bdes with ADOS I Corps & S.O.S.M. no 24 Light Workshop & Staff Captains of Bdes. Most of the wagons were badly in need of washers. Arranged programme of vehicles with S.O.M. for them to be sent in for various alterations.	
	14/9/16		Ordinary Routine work.	
	15/9/16		Had 12 cylinders of gas dumped into my store without my knowledge & went to look for another dump, not so near the station. 2 shells fell near the Dump.	
	16/9/16		Sent the Gas Cylinders out to Gas Officer at Divisional School. Nothing suitable to be had. Must stick it out.	
	17/9/16		Ordinary Routine work. No shells.	
	18/9/16		Took some Rifle grenade aiming rests for repair to no 24 Adv. S.S. Rifle with telescopic sights to Sniping School for repair.	

WAR DIARY
or
INTELLIGENCE SUMMARY

(Erase heading not required.)

Army Form C. 2118

Place	Date	Hour	Summary of Events and Information	Remarks and references to Appendices
In the Field	19/8/16.		Ordinary Routine work.	
	20/8/16.		Visited 90th Field Ambulance. Ordinary Routine work.	
	21/8/16.		Received 192 Pistols, holsters for No.1 & 2 Machine Gunners. Nothing further to report except the daily complement of shells which are getting very close to the Dump.	
	22/8/16.		Ordinary Routine work.	
	23/8/16.		Received new Lewis Gun for 15th H.L.I. Proceeded to Arrens for local purchase for Divn H.Q.s.	
	24/8/16.		Inspected with L.O.M. No 24 Workshop the transport vehicles of the 14 H.L.I. Bde. D.A.C. & G.O.C. of 32 Divnl Train. In need of interior except for wakening of wheels.	
	25/8/16.		Went to No 1 Heavy Ordnance Workshops to bring back sundry stores. Dump heavily shelled but not actually hit & two casualties. Decided to move the Dump.	

WAR DIARY or INTELLIGENCE SUMMARY

Army Form C. 2118

Place	Date	Hour	Summary of Events and Information	Remarks and references to Appendices
In the Field	26/8/16		Spent morning looking for new premises. Found some fairly suitable. Began move at once so as to try & finish before the regulation shelling begins. Got everything away but smoke helmets. Can move these in the morning.	
	27/8/16		Town heavily shelled last night. Shells very unpleasant as to where they fell. No damage to ordnance stores or personnel. A.D.O.S. I Corps paid a flying visit to new premises.	
	28/8/16		Visited all Battery wagon lines of 161 and 155 Bdes. Found no complaints as to supplies of ordnance stores. Ordinary routine work.	
	29/8/16		Visited Quartermasters wagon lines of 97th Bde. All satisfied, no complaints. Visited Divnl Laundry. Very efficient staff & the best managed Laundry I have seen yet.	
	30/8/16		Visited Lorn. No 24 workshop a repairs to vehicles etc & on to A.D.O.S. I Corps. Not at home.	

Place	Date	Hour	Summary of Events and Information	Remarks and references to Appendices
In the field	31/8/16		Routine work all morning. Took snipers Rifle to Sniping School to Repair & visited A.D.S. I Corps in the afternoon.	

M Urquhart Capt
DADVS 32 Div

Confidential

Vol 6

September 1916.

War Diary
— of —
D.A.D.O.S.
32nd Division.

No 6

Volume 1

Army Form C. 2118

WAR DIARY
or
INTELLIGENCE SUMMARY
(Erase heading not required.)

Instructions regarding War Diaries and Intelligence Summaries are contained in F.S. Regs, Part II. and the Staff Manual respectively. Title Pages will be prepared in manuscript.

Place	Date	Hour	Summary of Events and Information	Remarks and references to Appendices
In the Field	1/9/16		Went on leave. A few shells fell in the town last night.	
	7/9/16		Received 1 - 18 pr Gun for 4 168 Bde.	
	8/9/16		Received one 2" Trench Mortar fitted with Temple Silencer for issue on trial.	
	9/9/16		Received 8 Wagons - Limbered G.S. for issue to Train in lieu of 8 G.S. Wagons. Also received 1476 prs of Gum Boots Thigh as French Stores & 800 Tank Buckets for special occasion.	
	11/9/16		Received 1404 prs Gum Boots Thigh and 3200 Blankets. Returned to duty from leave.	
	12/9/16		Received 1128 prs Gum Boots Thigh and 4008 prs other kinds. Received 1800 prs of Puttees & formed Trench Foot Reserve to issue as change for both coming out of the Trenches.	
	13/9/16		Received 41 Handcarts for Lewis Guns and 2050 Blankets. Visited by A.D.O.S. I Corps.	
	14/9/16		Received 6 Hand carts for Lewis Guns and 2900 Blankets.	
	15/9/16		Received 1500 Blankets and no Lewis Gun for 15" Lewis Fuzi.	

F.W.M.

WAR DIARY
or
INTELLIGENCE SUMMARY.
(Erase heading not required.)

Army Form C. 2118.

Place	Date	Hour	Summary of Events and Information	Remarks and references to Appendices
In the Field	16/9/16		Received 2400 Blankets	
	17/9/16		Received 1800 Blankets. Two dial sights for 9.45 Trench mortar tried urgent. Also 595 prs of field service boots.	
	18/9/16		Received 2650 Blankets. Trench & Heavy Pistole Shop B.get - 3 Thornton Horn cylinders charged.	
	19/9/16		Received 300 Blankets. Sent to No 24 Light Workshop to arrange to supply of Rifle mechanism for Trench mortars & both 12 unserviceable Rifles to be made up for this purpose. Very important work can will be done.	
	20/9/16		Ordinary Routine work.	
	21/9/16		Received 1500 Blankets which complete 1st issue also 3992 prs of soles inner for Gum Boots. Went to No 24 shops to get 2 Rifle Rests & found the work well in hand & for the 2 required.	
	22/9/16		Received 2600 prs of soles inner also 9 Truple Silencers for 2" T.M. Tent & Heavy Postile Shop to change 2 Thornton Cylinders & got an adaptor made for the Pressure Gauge for Gas Cylinders.	W.W.

WAR DIARY
or
INTELLIGENCE SUMMARY.

(Erase heading not required.)

Army Form C. 2118.

Place	Date	Hour	Summary of Events and Information	Remarks and references to Appendices
In the field	23/9/16		Went to Henville & Estaires, for direct Purchase of Hammers & Claw Entract (nails) enough local purchase very difficult in this district.	
	24/9/16		Visited by Lt Longhurst ADO from G.H.Q to enquire into the requirement of Fuses, after withdrawal from Battle on the Somme. Was able to give the information required.	
	25/9/16		Ordinary Routine work. Visited Officers of Corps to arrange to supply of Underclothing for the Blighters.	
	26/9/16		Received one Vickers gun for 14 Mach. Gun Coy. Ordinary Routine work.	
	27/9/16		Received one 2" T.M. fuse rly for A 32 T.M.B. Went to Steen Werck Shops to ascertain if Muzzle Pivotings mountings (embodies) in this sector of the Line had been attended as they had been left by the Div: we had relieved. Also went on to Bu Workshops, got 4 Rifle Pucks for T.M. T.O.M. of this Shop is a splendid fellow & a glutton for work. Never refuses any thing to efficiency.	

W.P.L.

Army Form C. 2118.

WAR DIARY
or
INTELLIGENCE SUMMARY.
(Erase heading not required.)

Instructions regarding War Diaries and Intelligence Summaries are contained in F. S. Regs., Part II. and the Staff Manual respectively. Title pages will be prepared in manuscript.

Place	Date	Hour	Summary of Events and Information	Remarks and references to Appendices
In the Field	28/9/16		Ordinary Routine work. Nothing of importance to note.	
	29/9/16		Went to Henry Natale Shops also to Aire for Local purchase. Nothing further out of the ordinary Routine.	
	30/9/16		In office all day getting off Monthly Returns Inspection & War Diary. Visited by DADOS 6th Div. who wished to see how the fitting of new springs to lorries magnetos was being done the are the only division doing this work.	

F.W. Urquhart Capt.
DADOS 32 Divn

T1434. Wt. W708-776. 50C000. 4/15. Sir J. C. & S.

D.A.D.O.S.,

   32nd Division.

       War Diary returned for initials of
Officer signing at foot of each page.

Head Quarters.   Lieut. Colonel,
1st Oct. '16.   A.A. & Q.M.G., 32nd Division.

32 vol 7

~~DADOS~~

Confidential.

War Diary
— OF —
D. A. D. O. S.
32 Division.

Volume 1

N° 7

Army Form C. 2118.

WAR DIARY
or
INTELLIGENCE SUMMARY.
(Erase heading not required.)

Instructions regarding War Diaries and Intelligence Summaries are contained in F.S. Regs., Part II. and the Staff Manual respectively. Title pages will be prepared in manuscript.

Place	Date	Hour	Summary of Events and Information	Remarks and references to Appendices
In The Field.	1/10/16		Ordinary Routine work.	
	2/10/16		Went to see A.D.O.S. I Corps to clear up several matters of difficulty & to urge the same from there of 1 set of Branding Irons to each Coy of the Divisional Train as the 4 sets allowed to the D.T.C. are not sufficient to do the work of the whole Division, was instructed to put the application thro' Supt A.S.C. Grs. This was done (event forward).	
	3/10/16		Visited by A.D.O.S. I Corps, taken by him to 40th Divn & see the work being done there. Found everything in good order & very elaborate but the D.V. has been sitting in the same quarters for several months under these circumstances was not to be wondered at. Lt. Edwards, Larence who had been sent to the Divn. for instruction accompanied us & was left to take over the duties of D.A.D.O.S. of 40th Divn during absence of its D.A.D.O.S. [illeg.]	

T2134. Wt. W708 —776. 50000. 4/15. Sir J. C. & S.

WAR DIARY or INTELLIGENCE SUMMARY

Army Form C. 2118

Place	Date	Hour	Summary of Events and Information	Remarks and references to Appendices
In The Field	4/10/16		Proceeded to Amiens to local Purchase. Received 10,000 seats & 20,100 Band's Body.	
	5/10/16		Visited by O.O. 1st Corps Troops acting for A.D.O.S. I Corps whilst on duty in England. Sent lorry to 3rd Div Ordnance & collected some surplus stores left there by that Div on leaving the Corps.	
	6/10/16		Nothing out of the ordinary routine.	
	7/10/16		Went to Heavy Mobile shops to hasten the fitting of Truple Silencers on to 3. 2" T.M's. These were promised for Tuesday morning.	
	8/10/16		Ordinary Routine work.	
	9/10/16		Received 12,000 Drawers flannel. Also one Lewis machine gun for 2nd K.O.Y.L.I.	

Army Form C. 2118.

WAR DIARY
or
INTELLIGENCE SUMMARY.
(Erase heading not required.)

Place	Date	Hour	Summary of Events and Information	Remarks and references to Appendices
In The Field	10/10/16		Sent Arm. to Heavy Mobile Shop to fit the 3.2" T.M's. fitted with Temple Silencers also 3 2" T.M's & 8 6 Rifle mechanism to that firm.	
	11/10/16		Received one 18 pr. gun (piece only) T.M 15.168 and lowered one for A.168 condemned for maximum scoring B3 1.0.19. Pte Haley one of my storemen received 28 days F.P. no 1 for insubordination. Sentence given by A.A. & Q.M.G. Applied to Base for another man in this place.	
	12/10/16		Went to see D.A.D.O.S. 21st Div & handed over gun barrels, & Temple stores on our being relieved by this sector by 21st Div. Also to Merville to hasten 2 more 2" T.M's being fitted with Temple Silencers.	
	13/10/16		Received the 2" T.M's from Heavy Mobile. Nothing out of ordinary routine to report.	
	14/10/16		Commenced loading shop stuff & surplus stores on trucks at Railhead for consignment to our new area & cleared up generally. Received one 18 pr. for A.168.	

T.2134. Wt. W708 –776. 500000. 4/15. Sir J. C. & S.

WAR DIARY
or
INTELLIGENCE SUMMARY.
(Erase heading not required.)

Army Form C. 2118.

Instructions regarding War Diaries and Intelligence Summaries are contained in F.S. Regs., Part II. and the Staff Manual respectively. Title pages will be prepared in manuscript.

Place	Date	Hour	Summary of Events and Information	Remarks and references to Appendices
h.K. Field.	15/10/16		Completed loading & despatched 7 trucks with 15 men in charge of A.-S.Sgt. Elkins to our new area. Visited by A.D.O.S. I Corps who went round & inspected the supply stores & shops & expressed his satisfaction with our work & state under his administration.	
	16/10/16		Proceeded on 1st days march to Chelers. No billets provided for my personnel. Found some after much difficulty & saw the men settled in as comfortably as possible after purchasing straw privately.	
	17/10/16		Proceeded on 2 days march to de Caurcy. Men provided for this time.	
	18/10/16		Proceeded on 3rd days march to Beauval. Very wet & disagreeable march.	
	19/10/16		Proceeded with the drive to Contay ahead of the Division to arrange. There was informed the move was cancelled etc. Our man to stop at Beauval. The billet I occupied not being required I asked permission from our to my stores were unloaded permission granted.	

Army Form C. 2118.

WAR DIARY
or
INTELLIGENCE SUMMARY.
(Erase heading not required.)

Instructions regarding War Diaries and Intelligence Summaries are contained in F. S. Regs., Part II. and the Staff Manual respectively. Title pages will be prepared in manuscript.

Place	Date	Hour	Summary of Events and Information	Remarks and references to Appendices
In the Field.	20/10/16.		Received wire from Div that we were to move into 5 Corps area on the 21st. Sat tight for the day & phoned through in the evening to know there was to proceed in the following day. Was informed the Div would join me in the morning. Glad I did not have hysterics to go back to Beuvral in the preceding day.	
	21/10/16.		Division arrived & also all my stores from Bethune & the 15th men with them. Lt Reford & all men had behaved well & no trouble with them. Left Reford & other motor to 97 T.M.B. Received me & other motor to 97 T.M.B. we were to	
	22/10/16.		Cleared all the trucks from Railhead & then head we were to proceed to Bouzencourt in the morning.	
	23/10/16.		Proceeded to Bouzencourt. Found I had been allotted a dog kennel for a store & no armourers or shoemakers shop, had to be satisfied with store as place was full. Found a place to accommodate shop & shoe shop. Reported to O that no efforts were being made to provide me with suitable accommodation wrung from	Vosh.

T/134. Wt. W708—776. 500000. 4/15. Sir J. C. & S.

WAR DIARY
or
INTELLIGENCE SUMMARY.
(Erase heading not required.)

Army Form C. 2118.

Place	Date	Hour	Summary of Events and Information	Remarks and references to Appendices
In the Field	23/10/16 contd.		to sheer carelessness. D.A.A.Q.M.G. came down next morning to see into things & was disgusted. This will probably have good effect in the future.	
	24/10/16		Received 4000 capes mountain. Every day by my to adapt the dog kennel tiny requirements & leaving all the stores we had brought down from Bethune.	
	25/10/16		Received 1 Vickers gun for 96 M.G. Coy also 3 stokes mortars for 96 T.M.B. Visited D.H.L. H.Q. which are up in the line. Several shells went over & unknown destination in our back area.	
	26/10/16		Proceeded to Amiens for local purchase of rope for packing fucking & shovels up into the front line.	
	27/10/16		Received 26 Lewis guns to complete Divn to 16/Inn Battn. also 200 Braviers also (20 machines have shipping. Railhead moved to Acheux.	
	28/10/16		Units very scattered & owing to difficulty of congestion of roads & find it very difficult to send stuff out to distant units.	

Army Form C. 2118.

WAR DIARY
or
INTELLIGENCE SUMMARY.
(Erase heading not required.)

Instructions regarding War Diaries and Intelligence Summaries are contained in F. S. Regs., Part II. and the Staff Manual respectively. Title pages will be prepared in manuscript.

Place	Date	Hour	Summary of Events and Information	Remarks and references to Appendices
In the Field	29/10/16		Received 1000 of the 2nd Blanket per man. Proceeded to Amiens in Local purchase.	
	30/10/16		Received 4000 Cover waterproof to Bonnets + T.O.S. and 6000 pr. Gloves worsted and 1515 prs of Field Service Boots	
	31/10/16		Received 10,000 coats wollen, 6000 drawers woollen, 1100 Blankets and 34 sets pack saddlery G.S. for medical services. Rode up to Divnl Hd. Q. We shall most likely 200 y⁵ away, from D.H.Q. + a dud also close. Came home on completion of business	

M Wigginton Capt
DADOS 32 Divn

Vol 8

Confidential.

War Diary

∽ OF ∽

D.A.D.O.S.
32ⁿᵈ Division.

Volume 1

Nº 8.

WAR DIARY
INTELLIGENCE SUMMARY

Army Form C. 2118.

Place	Date	Hour	Summary of Events and Information	Remarks and references to Appendices
In the Field	1/11/16		Received 10,500 prs of Gloves Fingerless, 31 prs Shields hand and 20 Lyon stoves. Despatched highest account and war diary for Oct. Also 8220 Jerkins leather and 60 Coats Sheepskin lined.	
	2/11/16		Received Blanket 3000 (2" per man) and Drawers Woollen 300.	
	3/11/16		Visited ADOS II Corps and Divn A.Q.D at Verne still being heavily used & taking through the stores as received with having to clear Rail head, & take store to things in back area.	
	4/11/16		Received Drawers Woollen 8000 & Sweaters M.T. 200.	
	5/11/16		Received 200 Braces which completely finishes totals allotment of HOD. Proceeded to Amiens to local Purchase.	
	6/11/16		Nothing out of usual Routine Report.	
	7/11/16		Received 15 prs of Needles for night patrols.	
	8/11/16		Received 30 prs [?] for inglis patrols, 900 prs Braces Cotton Undercoats Fur 3390. Colt Sheepskin lined 22.	
	9/11/16		Went over to Divn H.Q. at Verne still where we to arrange training for making contract to supply of Linens prochainelles to shells later.	

WAR DIARY
or
INTELLIGENCE SUMMARY.
(Erase heading not required.)

Army Form C. 2118.

Place	Date	Hour	Summary of Events and Information	Remarks and references to Appendices
In the Field	10/10/16.		Proceeded to Amiens for local purchase of Rope for packs which was urgently required.	
	11/10/16.		Proceeded to Amiens to get the Canvas peakshades. Got 100 & paid for them at rate of 70.50 each. Much cheaper than was expected to the extent and that they were not so broad. 20 pm each.	
	12/10/16.		Issued the packs to 14 hy Bde for trial. They were not very suitable for lorries but quite good for shells. U. S. shrapnel.	
	13/10/16.		Received overalls for night patrols 75, boots F. S. 30 pair & socks Genuinenness long 2306.	
	14/10/16.		Nothing out of usual routine to report.	
	15/10/16.		Received 15 Iuronnerel stoves in lieu of Beatrice stoves very badly packed and 9 of them broken. Also 100 sets of Packsaddlery G. S. 48 pistols signal for M. G. coys and 139 cups for using on 23 Rifle Grenades.	
	16/10/16.		Proceeded to Amiens to purchase oil stoves for heating H.Q. Offices at camp in Vaux Hill.	

WAR DIARY
or
INTELLIGENCE SUMMARY

(Erase heading not required.)

Army Form C. 2118.

Instructions regarding War Diaries and Intelligence Summaries are contained in F. S. Regs., Part II. and the Staff Manual respectively. Title pages will be prepared in manuscript.

Place	Date	Hour	Summary of Events and Information	Remarks and references to Appendices
In the Field	16/11/16		Could only obtain two in all Armies.	
	17/11/16		Moved from Procurement & came under orders of the 5th Corps. Called to see the A.D.O.S. & get general instructions.	
	18/11/16		Proceeded to Armiens to purchase nose bags under orders of A.D.O.S. V Corps on Base was unable to supply at present. Purchased 500 of poor quality for 1-50 each. all that were obtainable. Further 500 to be ready by Thursday next. Also got the other 200 canvas haversacks at 12-50 each of slightly different pattern but suitable for carrying rations.	
	19/11/16		Nothing out of usual Routine to report.	
	20/11/16		Proceeded to Abbeville to make contract for nut hay under orders of D.D.V.S. V Corps as Base was unable to supply. Made contract for 5000 at 98 francs per 100s to be delivered between 20/11/16 and 15/12/16. Received from Base Boots F.S. 186 prs, Shorts A.B. 52 prs, Cords Sheepskin Lined 4,15, Gloves M.T. 130 prs, and Undercoats Fur 810.	

WAR DIARY or INTELLIGENCE SUMMARY

Army Form C. 2118.

Place	Date	Hour	Summary of Events and Information	Remarks and references to Appendices
In The Field	21/11/16		Nothing out of usual Routine to report.	
	22/11/16		Received two indents for Hosted Rations and 2000 F. Caps.	
	23/11/16		Proceeded to Amiens & bring out the other 500 nosebags & also sent 5 Lorry loads of stores from new destination.	
	24/11/16		Sent a further 4 lorry loads of stores from new destination & hope to clean up tomorrow when the Divisn move.	
	25/11/16		One lorry broke down in the night. Only 2 available to move the rest of the stores as one had to be left at new Railhead to clear. Finished then moved with D.H.Q. to Bullens ran to Canaples in the afternoon. Found (no) Store shops staff all settled in (returned) to Bulleny.	
	26/11/16		Found on reaching Canaples that all stores had been cleared from Berhancourt. The two lorries having made an extra trip in the night to clean the job up. Received from Base Sales Annex 6520 prs. Shirts 3000, Drawers 3000, Vests 2000, Socks 2100,	

Army Form C. 2118.

WAR DIARY
or
INTELLIGENCE SUMMARY.
(Erase heading not required.)

Instructions regarding War Diaries and Intelligence Summaries are contained in F. S. Regs., Part II. and the Staff Manual respectively. Title pages will be prepared in manuscript.

Place	Date	Hour	Summary of Events and Information	Remarks and references to Appendices
In the Field	27/11/16		Got the shops started to work everything in working order very good shops store this time plenty of room to work. Received 550 Nose Bags & 4080 Hay nets, and also 290 lamps F.S. to truck area also 500 Tubs washing.	
	28/11/16		Received 8400 Blankets from Base + rated 14 + 97th Bde 400 Pr. 6000 flue heated also came up.	
	29/11/16		Proceeded to Amiens to local purchase. No stores up from Base.	
	30/11/16		Received 210 lamps F.S. to complete to 500 to truck area also 2500 Rugs Horse.	

Murquhart Capt
DADOS 32 Div

T2134. Wt. W708—776. 50C000. 4/15. Sir J. C. & S.

Confidential.

Vol 9.

December 1916.

War Diary of

D.A.D.O.S.,

32nd Division.

No 9

Volume 1.

Army Form C. 2118.

WAR DIARY
or
INTELLIGENCE SUMMARY.
(Erase heading not required.)

Instructions regarding War Diaries and Intelligence Summaries are contained in F.S. Regs., Part II. and the Staff Manual respectively. Title pages will be prepared in manuscript.

Place	Date	Hour	Summary of Events and Information	Remarks and references to Appendices
In the Field.	1/12/16.		Proceeded to Bureau for local Purchase. No stores received from Base this day.	
	2/12/16.		Proceeded to Shipwreck Bay to cancel contract for 5000 hay nets as supplies are now coming up from Base. Proprietor was out — could do nothing till tomorrow. Visited T.C.P. who inspected store & shops received certified. Received 6300 Blankets G.S. from Base. also 1 18pr complete for C. 168 & one 4-5" How with carriage without B.M. to C-155 also 2 maltese carts for Signal Coy. with harness. Last of 3 due up.	
	3/12/16.		Received 7018 pr Shoes Horse & Mule. Primary Routine work. 2000 pr Drawers Woollen — 2000 Boots also 905 pr Boots Mule. Went to Raithes & afforded the 4-5" How for C-155 and one 18pr to C-168. also 200 Blankets to complete to 2 per man.	
	4/12/16.		Went to Shipwreck & succeeded in cancelling half the contract for haynets & bought back 1000 with me the remaining 1500 are to be ready by the 15/12/16.	

T.J. 134. Wt. W 708—776. 500000. 4/15. Sir J. C. & S.

Army Form C. 2118.

WAR DIARY
or
INTELLIGENCE SUMMARY.
(Erase heading not required.)

Instructions regarding War Diaries and Intelligence Summaries are contained in F.S. Regs., Part II. and the Staff Manual respectively. Title pages will be prepared in manuscript.

Place	Date	Hour	Summary of Events and Information	Remarks and references to Appendices
In The Field	5/12/16		Received a large consignment of General Stores and 100 Braziers + also 20 Flyers Stoves.	
	6/12/16		Received large quantities of Service Dress Clothing and also 7200 p/m Socks and 2500.	
	7/12/16		Went to Rouen to explain demands for underclothing, as there are no arrangements for laundry in this area. Received 1754 p/m of Boots Ankle.	
	8/12/16		Received large quantities of General Stores including Equipment etc. Went to Amiens on local purchase. Received to Stores Flyers to complete to 60 per Div. and 3400 p/m of Shoes House & Mule.	
	9/12/16		Received 330 p/m F.S. Boots and 3500 shirts. 5100 socks. 3000 vests. 3000 drawers together with other stores S.D. Clothing.	
	10/12/16		Received large supply of accessories and picketing gear also 1500 Bags mos.	
				KM.

Army Form C. 2118

WAR DIARY
or
INTELLIGENCE SUMMARY
(Erase heading not required.)

Place	Date	Hour	Summary of Events and Information	Remarks and references to Appendices
In The Field	12/12/16		Received 714 cases of small Box Respirators & 8 Lewis Guns for 11th Borders & two Vickers guns for 14th Bde M.G. Coy which had been on the way for nearly 3 weeks.	
	13/12/16		Proceeded to Amiens in the morning for local purchase & inspected 96 hy Bde in the afternoon & arranged for issue of clean underclothing (700 sets) for new Bath House just opened there.	
	14/12/16		Went with C.I.O.M. I Army to inspect the Transport of the 5/6 Royal Scots & arranged to send it to "Loris" at Beauqueme & Lucengue Tortworth. Received 1120 Box Respirators & Bulk oil frame & Stabling & 22 wheels.	
	15/12/16		Received 4 chaff cutting machines and 1966 prs of Shoes Horse and Mule & 680 Broom Bass for Area Stores.	
	16/12/16		Received S.D. Clothing & 4000 Vests & 4000 Drawers & 500 prs Boots Ankle.	

MM.

Army Form C. 2118

WAR DIARY
or
INTELLIGENCE SUMMARY
(Erase heading not required.)

Instructions regarding War Diaries and Intelligence Summaries are contained in F.S. Regs., Part II. and the Staff Manual respectively. Title Pages will be prepared in manuscript.

Place	Date	Hour	Summary of Events and Information	Remarks and references to Appendices
In The Field	17/12/16		Received fresh supply of Rotating Fan General Stores also 2000 Small Box Respirators. 1. Refitted H.Q. R.S. & D.A.C. 150 O.Rs of the Train. 2. Visited H.Q. of the Train.	
	18/12/16		Received large Quantity of Necessaries and 4000 shirts and 2100 pr socks. Proceeded to Amiens on Local Purchase.	
	19/12/16		Received Eng.List Truck of Horse Shoes which has been on the road for 2 weeks having left Havre on Oct. 30th. Reported its arrival to Corps & Army as directed. This is the last of the delayed Trucks.	
	20/12/16		Arranged for Temporary Dump at Railhead in case of Road Precautions being enforced. No stores from Base today.	
	21/12/16		Proceeded on Leave to England.	

McStephens Capt
D.A.D.O.S 32nd Div

Confidential.

January 1917.

War Diary

— of —

D.A.D.O.S.,

32nd Division.

No. 4

Volume 2.

WAR DIARY
or
INTELLIGENCE SUMMARY
(Erase heading not required.)

Army Form C. 2118

Place	Date	Hour	Summary of Events and Information	Remarks and references to Appendices
In The Field	1/1/17.		Arrived at Divl HdQrs after 10 days leave of absence.	
	2/1/17.		No stores from Base today. Sent off Supplies Account and War Diary for December. Spent the whole day picking up the threads accumulated in my absence. Everything had gone well & Chief Clerk had carried on very satisfactorily.	
	3/1/17.		Received large consignment of U.S. Clothing & 869 pr boot ankle, also 2000 shirt, Drawers woollen & socks.	
	4/1/17.		Went in lorry to see A.D.O.S. of Corps re need of walk trch. Sent on some of the things to Bern where we are to take over from 3's Divn.	
	5/1/17.		Sent over 4 more lorry loads of things etc to Bern	
	6/1/17.		Cleared all stores from Cauroples except one load incld underclothing which is to go to Virgin court in the morning in trks into Divl HdQrs to Marieux.	
	7/1/17.		Received further supplies of S.D. Clothing stone ecc, drawing on grease. Very heavy day for the stores staff.	
	8/1/17.		Went to Bern & inspected stores offices now that all was in working order, preparatory to moving over the next day.	

Army Form C. 2118

WAR DIARY
or
INTELLIGENCE SUMMARY
(Erase heading not required.)

Instructions regarding War Diaries and Intelligence Summaries are contained in F. S. Regs., Part II. and the Staff Manual respectively. Title Pages will be prepared in manuscript.

Place	Date	Hour	Summary of Events and Information	Remarks and references to Appendices
In the Field	9/1/17		Moved on to Bus with Divl HQrs. No stores from Base this day.	
	10/1/17		Received supplies of 60 ft fuse necessary. Went to Amiens & purchase 500 hose bags urgently required as none had been received from Base for 3 weeks. Full demands up.	
	11/1/17		2500 nosebags came up today. 'Of course' they would! Tested 4.5 Gr by of Field Trans & 4.5" Q.F. artillery & also 29 CT workshop.	
	12/1/17		Proceeded to Amiens to purchase white metal and Babbets for making spt Ford Containers under instructions from Divl Commander.	
	13/1/17		Received 1829 prs shoe horse & mule. 120 Zinc stirk Jars & 1000 blankets.	
	14/1/17		Received food supply of S.D. Anthony & 4000 feets & Brewers trouth to replace similar number sent to Paris duty.	

V. Will

WAR DIARY or INTELLIGENCE SUMMARY

Army Form C. 2118

(Erase heading not required.)

Instructions regarding War Diaries and Intelligence Summaries are contained in F.S. Regs., Part II. and the Staff Manual respectively. Title Pages will be prepared in manuscript.

Place	Date	Hour	Summary of Events and Information	Remarks and references to Appendices
In the Field.	15/1/17		Received Rotating Saw including 2400 rise tugs, footed Transport of 14s and 96 bdes + rain 2 M.T. no complaints.	
	16/1/17		Received 4000 shrifs + 6300 pm rope + fort supply of necessaries. Proceeded to Bruens to purchase sheet & potatoes. Not available.	
	17/1/17		Collected Store Tent from Beaucourt took it to Bodle & used for dumping stores in case of R+D precautions. 6 inches of snow fell during night. In office all day except for going round to the shops + stores. Feeling cold.	
	18/1/17		Boots to Bde up from Base today. Collected 300 butter jerkins from C.O. I Corp Troops. Still snowing.	
	19/1/17		Received Bulk Dubbin, oil + grease and 1950 Bore Reprieds for Divie Reserve.	
	20/1/17		Received Bulk Horse + Mule shoes and 30 Vacuum Bulk which latter were handed over to Divie Gas Officer.	W.W.

Army Form C. 2118

WAR DIARY
or
INTELLIGENCE SUMMARY
(Erase heading not required.)

Instructions regarding War Diaries and Intelligence Summaries are contained in F.S. Regs., Part II. and the Staff Manual respectively. Title Pages will be prepared in manuscript.

Place	Date	Hour	Summary of Events and Information	Remarks and references to Appendices
In the Field	21/1/17		Received Bulk Issue Frea Clothing. Very severe frost during the night. Visited by D.A.D.O.S. 62 Div. who is coming up to take over	
	22/1/17		Received Bulk picketing Gear etc. & 25 hr Goggles with Triplex Glasses which were issued, 8 to each Bgde, Bde & 1 to General Staff.	
	23/1/17		Moved over to Bertrancourt & handed over all the stores out of store to Railhead. Very severe frost and the lorries could not return till midday. Had to leave 4 numerous shop behind till next day as no lorries available. No stores from Base.	
	24/1/17		Walked over to Buo to superintend moving of numerous shop also to see Gum Boot Store which will have to stay where it is till some suitable place here can be found.	
	25/1/17		Received Bulk Ankle boots & Sundry etc. Walked over to S.A.A. Dump to locate it - to collect 29 prs hob-nail boots left there by I.A. Div. Collected same in the afternoon & handed over to J.B. 7 Corps troops as divided. Visited Railhead. Arranged for truck to despatch 2000 sets of dirty underclothing to Paris which cannot be washed here.	

JHL

WAR DIARY
or
INTELLIGENCE SUMMARY

(Erase heading not required.)

Army Form C. 2118

Place	Date	Hour	Summary of Events and Information	Remarks and references to Appendices
In the Field	26/1/17		Received 48/hr Traces were short in scale of 4 per Battery for adding traces horses to Ration wagons in the mud.	
	27/1/17		Got Bad cold cough feeling rotten, talked over & saw ADTS V Corps v O.C. V Corps Troops & arranged to draw some leather jerkins	
	28/1/17		Received Bush Hose & Mule Shoes & Picketing gear also 1st Patrol Trestley to replace losses v/t to several Units.	
	29/1/17		Attended conference of V.A.D.'s &c. at A.D.T.S. V Corps office to discuss the reorganisation of Divl Artillery Letter matter. Spent an hour with Staff Capt R.A. Straffing out the actual Surplus caused. Must also see the D.T.O. as soon as possible have got the that- of stores surplus on breaking up of C.153 now require the surplus of the D.T.O. on departure of section of H.A.C. to Army Brigade.	
	30/1/17		Visited O.C. 2. Manchester to ascertain what action had been taken re the loss of practically all their magazines Lewis Sun found strong deflationary action, many guns had been enfused & (none) sudent to the Base in action.	

Army Form C. 2118

WAR DIARY
or
INTELLIGENCE SUMMARY
(Erase heading not required.)

Place	Date	Hour	Summary of Events and Information	Remarks and references to Appendices
In The Field	31/8/17		Proceeded to Amiens for local purchase. Called in to see A.D.V.S. V Corps on the way & took Pattern Hot Food Container to Army (I) Q. for inspection. It was well thought of & returned for purpose of showing to Army Commander. Called at A.D.V.S. office on way back & picked up the Instructors for Numn. Dumps.	

Murquhart Capt
D.A.D.V.S. 32 Divn

Confidential.

Vol XI

War Diary.

~ of ~

D.A.D.O.S,

32nd Division.

Volume 2.

No 2.

Army Form C. 2118

WAR DIARY
or
INTELLIGENCE SUMMARY
(Erase heading not required.)

Place	Date	Hour	Summary of Events and Information	Remarks and references to Appendices
In the field	1/2/19		Received Dubbin, oil & grease & equipment from Base, also 24 Lewis Gun to increase scale to 14 per Battalion. 1056 magazines came with the Guns.	
	2/2/19		Received Buck Horse Shoes etc from Base. Proceeded to Amiens for Local purchase. Made up 25 Rocket Crews in Amiens Shop	
	3/2/19		Received Buck Accessories, Grinders. Went over to see D.A.D.O.S. 62 Bon transit in any way that I could.	
	4/2/19		Received 1275 Blankets as 3 's in war for Troops under Canvas also Service Dress Clothing & Boots.	
	5/2/19		Went to Railhead & Salvage Dump. Received Picketing Gear & several stores.	
	6/2/19		Received ne 18th from Gun for D.168 Bde R.F.A. No other stores. Proceeded to Amiens to order 500 whistles enough for attaching troops to be ready by noon on the 8th. Made contact at store each with Vagney & Seminel of Amiens.	W.W.

WAR DIARY
or
INTELLIGENCE SUMMARY

Army Form C. 2118

Place	Date	Hour	Summary of Events and Information	Remarks and references to Appendices
In the Field	7/2/17.		Had to countermand order for white duncks as Army refused to authorise purchase. Later in day authority was given to purchase to zero on the 9th. Receive Boots ankle + 1000 shirts.	
	8/2/17.		Received 1250 steel Helmets with chain visors issued all to 97 Bde for their attack.	
	9/2/17.		Received Sulphic oil. Grease necessaries. Went to Armentières & brought back the white smocks. Delivered direct to 97 Bde.	
	10/2/17.		Railhead shifted to Belle Eglise. Engine no stores from Base. Railhead 3 officers + 215 stores captured). attack complete success.	
	11/2/17.		Received S.D. Clothing + Sundery. Went to see Depots 62 Div to arrange about handing over stores in relief.	
	12/2/17.		Received picketing Gear + Horse Shoes. Sorted out the pile of packsaddlery left by J Div + carefully checked it made up as far as possible + referred result to A.D.O.S. I Corps.	
	13/2/17.		Received further supply of picketing gear + equipment.	

Army Form C. 2118

WAR DIARY
or
INTELLIGENCE SUMMARY
(Erase heading not required.)

Place	Date	Hour	Summary of Events and Information	Remarks and references to Appendices
In The Field	14/2/17		Cancelled stores from Base in new Division moving. Handed over the Archaddley to "2" Bn. Delivered 1. to Bn. Took o/c Gum Boots of 62" Bn. moved the Gum Boot store & arranged for handing over.	
	15/2/17		Received the Gum Store for 15" H.L.I. in total Truck & went to see Billets allotted use in new area.	
	16/2/17		Handed over Gum Boots & all other area stores to 62" Bn.	
	17/2/17		Moved to Villers Bocage.	
	18/2/17		Received Shoe Horses, mule, oiling oil, grease etc & me issued same for "2" Manchester Regt.	
	19/2/17		Rode over to Mann to see C.R.A. & D.A.C.	
	20/2/17		Went to see Billets allotted in new area & despatched the Shops & some stores in 8 lorries to destination with all ships reserved.	
	21/2/17		Moved to be Quesnel.	
	22/2/17		Settled down & got all shops going. Collected with assistance of 12 lorries from Corps 6000 prs Gum Boots & other area stores from to Corps Railhead, Roads awful.	WW

Army Form C. 2118

WAR DIARY
or
INTELLIGENCE SUMMARY
(Erase heading not required.)

Instructions regarding War Diaries and Intelligence Summaries are contained in F.S. Regs., Part II. and the Staff Manual respectively. Title Pages will be prepared in manuscript.

Place	Date	Hour	Summary of Events and Information	Remarks and references to Appendices
In the Field	23/2/17		Collected further area stores from 4 Corps Railhead also no own, including 4 chaff cutters.	
	24/2/17		Received 2 Lewis Guns for 2" Hag L.I. and 2 for the 16 N.F.; also 1 chaff cutter & 7000 dismountans locks. Proceeded Amiens for local purchase. Railhead shifted to Mericies.	
	25/2/17		Rode to Railhead but no truck for us today.	
	26/2/17		Received one lorry load from 17 A.D.S. no other stores.	
	27/2/17		Visited 97 Inf Bde H.Q. Proceeded to Amiens & 4 Army H.Qrs & Heavy Motile Workshops & Rouen Dual Light for repair.	
	28/2/17		Visited A.D.S. 4 Corps. Received 4000 shirts, 4200 socks & 3800 rats from Base.	

Munguhar Capt
D.A.D.S. 32" Br

1875 Wt. W593/826 1,000,000 4/15 J.B.C. & A. A.D.S.S./Forms/C.2118.

Confidential.　　　　　March 1917.

No 12

War Diary
~ of ~
D. A. D. O. S.,
32 Division.

Volume 2.

Nº 3.

Army Form C. 2118

WAR DIARY
or
INTELLIGENCE SUMMARY
(Erase heading not required.)

Instructions regarding War Diaries and Intelligence Summaries are contained in F.S. Regs., Part II and the Staff Manual respectively. Title Pages will be prepared in manuscript.

Place	Date	Hour	Summary of Events and Information	Remarks and references to Appendices
In The Field.	1/3/17.		Went to Corps Headquarters & Railhead. Received Boots & necessaries also 4000 shirts, 3600 vests, 4200 socks from Aux. Horse. From Havre received Infys new set Equipment & Outfits of Drum.	
	2/3/17.		Visited sock laundry in the morning & BTO & H.Q. Cy. of Divnl Train in the afternoon. Received 1 Lewis Gun for 16 Lancers & some clothes morters for 97 - T.M.B. also picketing gear.	
	3/3/17.		Went to Heavy mobile shop store & 2" mortar & to futto with adopter & 4 durrys. Breech mechanism got to new in exchange. Returned thru Amiens to local Produce. Received S.D. Clothing from Base.	
	4/3/17.		Received 2000 Box Respirators from Base. Visited 96 Inf Bde in the afternoon.	
	5/3/17.		No stores from Base but we drew 200H per Sum boots Thigh from 4 Corps Troops. Visited Divnl Baret Store with DA QMG & tried a Vickers Gun repaired in armourers shop before issue. Examined all detail returns outstanding arranged for cancellation or statutory action to be taken.	Mir

Army Form C. 2118.

WAR DIARY
or
INTELLIGENCE SUMMARY
(Erase heading not required.)

Instructions regarding War Diaries and Intelligence Summaries are contained in F. S. Regs., Part II. and the Staff Manual respectively. Title Pages will be prepared in manuscript.

Place	Date	Hour	Summary of Events and Information	Remarks and references to Appendices
In the Field	6/3/17		Received a truck of General stores very satisfactory supply of detail stores. Stage an enemy is wonderfully well all work are well satisfied. Proceeded to Amiens for Urgent Local Purchase in the afternoon.	
	7/3/17		Received Boots. Received 4000 Shirts & Socks from Base. Went to Army Mobile shops fitting back 1. 2" T.M + 6 rifle mechanisms.	
	8/3/17		Went to Railhead. No stores up from base. Went on to A.D.O.S. IV Corps to urge the issue of Packsaddlery in case of active operation.	
	9/3/17		Received 41 wheels. Bulk Horse shoes, draftbay of races. Also 1 water cart + 1 limbered G.S. Wagon for 5/6 Royal Scots & 15" H.L.I.	
	10/3/17		Received Bulk clothing & went to Amiens for Local Purchase.	
	11/3/17		Received Bulk General Stores, some Regimentals steel helmets 5 wheels.	
	12/3/17		Went to Amiens for Local Purchase. No stores from Base.	M.M.

2449 Wt. W14957/M90 750,000 1/16 J.B.C. & A. Forms/C.2118/12.

Army Form C. 2118.

WAR DIARY
or
INTELLIGENCE SUMMARY
(Erase heading not required.)

Instructions regarding War Diaries and Intelligence Summaries are contained in F. S. Regs., Part II. and the Staff Manual respectively. Title Pages will be prepared in manuscript.

Place	Date	Hour	Summary of Events and Information	Remarks and references to Appendices
In The Field	13/3/17.		Received 7 cycles, 12 wheels, Bulk wastage etc. Wired 1 om 2s 28 workshop to take 2 2" TMs for repair.	
	14/3/17.		Received 7 tons Bulk Clothing.	
	15/3/17.		Received Bulk Battery, oil & grease. Made arrangements for Ordnance services in case of an advance.	
	16/3/17		Received 13 wheels, Bulk Horse Shoes & Rugs, Hose also 1 trolley kitchen for 15 H.L.I.	
	17/3/17.		Received 100 sets of Packsaddlery. Bulk clothing. Severe attacks & found Boche had evacuated his line & made a considerable advance. Sent out W.O's & filling point with their storemen & clerks on the lorries, so as to effect a hasty liaison. Distribution of Bulk stores to be made in Truck at (Railhead).	
	18/3/17.		Went to Railhead, made distribution of Bulk, several stores normally moved with D.H.Q. & travellers brought in reserve of 15 mo. Regimentis stock.	

Army Form C. 2118.

WAR DIARY
or
INTELLIGENCE SUMMARY

(Erase heading not required.)

Instructions regarding War Diaries and Intelligence Summaries are contained in F. S. Regs., Part II. and the Staff Manual respectively. Title Pages will be prepared in manuscript.

Place	Date	Hour	Summary of Events and Information	Remarks and references to Appendices
In The Field.	19/3/17.		Received Box respirators + Steel helmets + 138 horses. As the Division is rapidly advancing, returned the Box Respirators + Braziers as reserve of former was complete. Moved with D.H.Q. to Daucourt.	
	20/3/17.		No Stores from Base. Moved to Neale, brought reserves in Roads very bad + horses working all night to get the Reserve up. (Reserve) 500 Trench covers.	
	21/3/17.		Went to Railhead. No Stores. Horses very difficult but have managed to issue all stores every Day. System working very smoothly.	
	22/3/17.		Received 41 wheels, Bulk dubbing. Got part of the ships moved up to Neale. No extra transport available.	
	23/3/17.		Went to Railhead, made distribution of Bulk Horse Shoes.	
	24/3/17.		Went to Railhead as usual received + distributed Bulk clothing.	
	25/3/17.		Went to Railhead. No stores. Moved balance of ships up to Neale.	

Army Form C. 2118.

WAR DIARY
or
INTELLIGENCE SUMMARY

(Erase heading not required.)

Instructions regarding War Diaries and Intelligence Summaries are contained in F. S. Regs., Part II. and the Staff Manual respectively. Title Pages will be prepared in manuscript.

Place	Date	Hour	Summary of Events and Information	Remarks and references to Appendices
In the Field	26/3/17		No Store. Went to Amiens for local purchases.	
	27/3/17.		Went to Railhead. 11 Wheel & Bulk Several Stores. All stores are being issued regularly & satisfactorily in supply wagon from Refilling Point.	
	28/3/17.		Railhead as usual. Bulk Clothing. arranged for move to during the next day.	
	29/3/17.		Moved Railhead. For the 1st time since advance began. Received 38 Wheels. Bulk Sulphur, Oil & grease & 2n down from to supply the Divn to 16 Apr Battn. Also 48 pistols for Machine Gunners. Moved to Aubin.	
	30/3/17.		Got some of the shops moved to Vayenne variates refilling points. Received Bulk Horse shoes etc.	
	31/3/17.		Went to Railhead. 3 tons Bulk clothing. Completes move & Shops to Vayenne. Various refilling points. Brought up 20 Shrunks Horses from to Quesnel.	

W. Urquhart. Capt.
D.A.D.O.S. 32-Dn

31/3/17

Confidential.　　　　　　　　April 1917.

App 15

War Diary

OF

D.A.D.O.S.,

32 Division.

Volume 2.

No. 4.

Army Form C. 2118.

WAR DIARY
or
INTELLIGENCE SUMMARY

(Erase heading not required.)

Instructions regarding War Diaries and Intelligence Summaries are contained in F. S. Regs., Part II. and the Staff Manual respectively. Title Pages will be prepared in manuscript.

Place	Date	Hour	Summary of Events and Information	Remarks and references to Appendices
In the Field	1/4/17.		Visited Dump morning & afternoon. Railhead moves to Nosle tomorrow which will make things much easier.	
	2/4/17.		Went to Railhead as usual & rested thyo replying point in return journey. Everything working satisfactorily.	
	3/4/17.		Went to Railhead & on to Guesnel to ensure that nothing had been left behind that was likely to be required. Visited hp. at the Replying front in the evening.	
	4/4/17.		Railhead as usual. Ran to Guesnel for urgent local purchases.	
	5/4/17.		Sent lorry from 6 to Guesnel to get the white sugar for troops attacking in the finer under the loading hp. Visited replying front in the evening as usual.	
	6/4/17.		Ran to Peronne & contrived got to Rail head. It was a good thing I had insisted on duplicate copy of Bulk stock in case of emergency. One copy in charge of the Railhead conductor.	
	7/4/17.		Went to Railhead. No stores. Ran to Guesnel made instructions from O.R.little account for Brusschool. Called at Replying front in the Way back.	

WWC

Army Form C. 2118.

WAR DIARY
or
INTELLIGENCE SUMMARY

(Erase heading not required.)

Instructions regarding War Diaries and Intelligence Summaries are contained in F. S. Regs., Part II. and the Staff Manual respectively. Title Pages will be prepared in manuscript.

Place	Date	Hour	Summary of Events and Information	Remarks and references to Appendices
In the Field	8/4/17		Railhead & Dumps as usual. Rode out to see Staff Capt. 14 Bde. Saw French kite Balloon set on fire + brought down by Bosche airman. Had in to Bors Motor to see D'Quentin. Bosche plane destroyed on way home.	
	9/4/17		One Bosche down again, could not get to Railhead at all. Cheery up in lot of office work. Heard splendid news of an offensive in the North.	
	10/4/17		Visited Railhead & Dumps as usual also saw O.C. D.A.C. Nothing of Importance known.	
	11/4/17		Visited Railhead A.D.O.S. & Dumps & also O.C. No 9 Cy. Train. Rode to 14 Bde HQrs in the afternoon	
	12/4/17		Railhead & Dumps. Received one Vickers Gun Jr 29 March from Coy.	
	13/4/17		Car in the workshop. Nothing. Routine work.	

Army Form C. 2118.

WAR DIARY
or
INTELLIGENCE SUMMARY
(Erase heading not required.)

Instructions regarding War Diaries and Intelligence Summaries are contained in F. S. Regs., Part II. and the Staff Manual respectively. Title Pages will be prepared in manuscript.

Place	Date	Hour	Summary of Events and Information	Remarks and references to Appendices
In The Field	14/4/17		Received 1 Vickers Gun for 96th M.G. Coy. Car still out of action.	
	15/4/17		Visited Railhead & Dump as Car was available. Talked seriously to R.T.O. who is trying to stop my doing the distribution of Stores in the truck at Railhead. Frightened him out.	
	16/4/17		Proceeded to Funcuio after Railhead for urgent local Purchase.	
	17/4/17		Q.M.S J. Artillery units not attending refilling point. R.A. Ordered them to do so regularly. Got the totally Captain A.D.O.S. & I.O. & Corps Troops also I.O.M. over sent ADS immediately.	
	18/4/17		Visited Railhead.	
	19/4/17		Applied for leave for the 23rd April. Four months since I went last time. Visited 97 Bde & O.C. supply Column.	
	20/4/17		Division to go out to rest on 22nd. Sent some of my store down.	
	21/4/17		Received 1 steam from for 2 Horses & 1 one token for 97 M.G. Coy. Rest over this afternoon.	
	22/4/17		Visited Railhead & started for Funcuio on leave.	

Murgulush Capt
& ADOS 32. .

Confidential   May 1917

Vol/14

War Diary

OF

D.A.D.O.S.

32 Division

Volume 2

No 5.

Army Form C. 2118

WAR DIARY
or
INTELLIGENCE SUMMARY
(Erase heading not required.)

Place	Date	Hour	Summary of Events and Information	Remarks and references to Appendices
In The Field	4/5/17		Arrived for duty at D.H.Q. after 10 days leave of absence.	
	5/5/17		Proceeded to Railhead & made all refilling points checks. Dispatched Urgent Cal. & War Diary for preceding month. Divisional Staff quite satisfied with conduct of affairs during my absence on leave.	
	6/5/17		Visited Railhead & all refilling points also Q.M. of 2" H.Q.v.c.y. Visited 96" Inf Bde in the afternoon.	
	7/5/17		Visited Railhead & proceeded to Amiens to enquire for urgent local Purchases. Received Bulk Horse Shoes for Div Registration. Also got Iv Ruts.	
	8/5/17		Visited Railhead & unp. as usual. Also got Iv Ruts. Received Gen. Store & 1 18 pr piece for B.168.	
	9/5/17		Visited Railhead & Divnl as usual received Bulk Boot-Ankle & Necessaries. Also instructions for S.168, 1 pr to S.161 & reorganisation of Travelling kitchens for S/6 Ryal Scots. Sport Staff with the afternoon. Ordnance Staff got 4 secnd divises.	

WAR DIARY or INTELLIGENCE SUMMARY

Army Form C. 2118

Place	Date	Hour	Summary of Events and Information	Remarks and references to Appendices
In The Field.	10/5/17		Posted Dumps & Railhead as usual. Received Buck Stretcher, oil & grease & Box Respirators & 118 ph pieces for B. 161.	
	11/5/17		Received Bulk Horse & Mule Shoes & nail, allotment of Champion, Farrier Helmets & tools for fixing them. Posted the Dumps as per B.800 G.W.	
	12/5/17		Received Brown Truck with Service Dress Clothing, Sundary & Necessaries. Despatched 4 Trucks of Blankets to Base. Suspended issues from Base in view of the prospective move.	
	13/5/17		Sent off two more trucks of Blankets & Jerkins to Base & re'd A.D.S.S. & Capt. & S.O. & Exp. Troop.	
	14/5/17		Sent off 3 more trucks of Winter Clothing to Base & had the Shop (Banker) up ready to go in the morning.	
	15/5/17		Sent off the Shops & Received some of our new appliances re'd the	
	16/5/17		Moved to Beaurevoir with D.amd ADQ". Found the shops all settled in at work.	
	17/5/17		Went to Amiens for Local Purchase. No stores up.	

Army Form C. 2118

WAR DIARY
or
INTELLIGENCE SUMMARY
(Erase heading not required.)

Instructions regarding War Diaries and Intelligence Summaries are contained in F.S. Regs., Part II. and the Staff Manual respectively. Title Pages will be prepared in manuscript.

Place	Date	Hour	Summary of Events and Information	Remarks and references to Appendices
In The Field	18/5/17		Received Truck of Hors Shoes, General Stores, Butter, oil & grease. Part of Railhead and dump "96" & "14" etc. not yet.	
	19/5/17		Received Rouen Truck with Clothing, Boots, Caps, Provisions. Started Dump Railhead & on to Arrivers to Q.	
	20/5/17		Received Truck of Equipment General Stores, rivetted all Dumps & "96" "B.M" not Q.	
	21/5/17		No stores & very little to do. Went for a ride & practiced on the range. Shooting rotten.	
	22/5/17		Received Truck of Equipment. Staff Respirators also initial issue of 650 P. Butter Machine Respirators.	
	23, 24 & 25/5/17		Nothing doing. Serviced at May Hall Brigade having sports etc. Distillery. O.P.C. & C.O. Team have left us for Autumn Destination. Students Manoeuvers of 2 Army Troops inspected Train.	
	26/5/17		Received Lack Truck from Rouen of Clothing Necessaries Boots Ankle etc. Went to Arrivers to Q.	

WM

WAR DIARY
or
INTELLIGENCE SUMMARY

(Erase heading not required.)

Army Form C. 2118

Instructions regarding War Diaries and Intelligence Summaries are contained in F. S. Regs., Part II. and the Staff Manual respectively. Title Pages will be prepared in manuscript.

Place	Date	Hour	Summary of Events and Information	Remarks and references to Appendices
In the Field	27/5/17		No stores. Nothing much to do. Had some revolver practise.	
	28/5/17		Nothing to report.	
	29/5/17		Loaded up 5 trucks with shops. Reserves & clean clothing. Sgt. Keith & shops personnel.	
	30/5/17		Sgt. Jas(?) set out with Army nothing & loaded up with Balance. After left at 9.45 to 2 Army Hers. Leaving my Sgt. Clerk to see to loading of 2" Blucker which are being taken to Ruitres by supply lorries. Arrived at Keurs Bergues at 2-30 p.m. (8th Bn HQ occupied) to shops etc. Fixed up hitched tent for the night. Shops etc arrived at Railhead at 3 p.m. & worked all night setting the truck cleared. Burned 2 lorries soda & help.	
	31/5/17			

MW Luches(?) Capt.
S.A.D.V.S. 32' Dan

Confidential   June 1917

Vol 15

War Diary
of
D.A.D.O.S.
32 Division.

Volume 2

Nº 6.

Army Form C. 2118

WAR DIARY
or
INTELLIGENCE SUMMARY
(Erase heading not required.)

Instructions regarding War Diaries and Intelligence Summaries are contained in F.S. Regs., Part II. and the Staff Manual respectively. Title Pages will be prepared in manuscript.

Place	Date	Hour	Summary of Events and Information	Remarks and references to Appendices
In The Field.	1/6/17		Went to Railhead but no truck up today. Went on to see A.D.S.T. XIV Corps & Field Cashier. Ordinary Routine Work. Divn H.Q. arrived during the day.	
	2/6/17		Went round & located the Refilling Points. Established the Bde H.Q.'s at their respective points. Went to Nesville to purchase some rope & arrange for the manufacture of some rifle grenade carriers.	
	3/6/17		Went to Railhead & Coys. When on to Hazebrouck & tried to get some rope. Succeeded in getting a little & handed by to C.R.E. truck slings for carrying petrol tins of water. Went to Calais base to get some churns for nothing. The	
	4/6/17		Proceeded to Calais base to get some churns for nothing. The Grenade carriers rely some rope. Ifl D.J. accompanied me. Took the Churns to the place in Nesville to be made up.	
	5/6/17		Visited 13th, 14th & 12th Bdes. refilling points. Went to Nesville to see how manufacture of carriers is progressing. No stores up.	

1875. Wt. W593/826 1,000,000 4/15 J.B.C. & A. A.D.S.S./Forms/C. 2118.

WAR DIARY
or
INTELLIGENCE SUMMARY

(Erase heading not required.)

Army Form C. 2118

Instructions regarding War Diaries and Intelligence Summaries are contained in F. S. Regs., Part II. and the Staff Manual respectively. Title Pages will be prepared in manuscript.

Place	Date	Hour	Summary of Events and Information	Remarks and references to Appendices
In The Field	6/6/17		Proceeded to Dumps as no stores were at Railhead. Collected 2 Lewis Gun from 5/6 Royal Scots for repair in Armourers Shop. Went in to A.D.O.S. Corps Stores from O. C. Corps Troops. 6 Lewis Stores, 10 Drums & 2500 anti-Drum outfits. Went to Perville in the afternoon & collected 900 grenade carriers locally made & issued them to the three Inf. Bdes. This completes them to 144 per Batt - as asked for. Received one 3" Stokes mortar to 96 T.M.B.	
	7/7/17.		Went to Railhead. Shells were falling not more than 150 yds away. Received 1 Vickers Gun to 97 M.G. Coy. Received 184 ack Packsaddles to complete Division to 300 set. Also General Stores.	
	8/7/17.		No stores except 1 3" Stokes mortar to 96 T.M.B. Visited Dumps.	
	9/7/17.		No stores. Received 150 large Cutters wire from Gun Park. Visited Dumps & A.D.O.S. & Corp. Routine work.	
	10/7/17.		No stores. Ordinary Routine work.	
	11/7/17.		Received 4 Tons General Stores + 100 Yukon Packs to complete the Division to 250.	
	12/7/17.		Visited new area selected site for Dumps. Four Lorry loads of Packsaddlery followed me up. Nothing satisfactory found so dumped Stores in Riddles Huts.	

1875. Wt. W593/826 1,000,000. 4/15 J.B.C. & A. A.D.S.S./Forms/C.2118.

Army Form C. 2118

WAR DIARY
or
INTELLIGENCE SUMMARY
(Erase heading not required.)

Instructions regarding War Diaries and Intelligence Summaries are contained in F. S. Regs., Part II. and the Staff Manual respectively. Title Pages will be prepared in manuscript.

Place	Date	Hour	Summary of Events and Information	Remarks and references to Appendices
In The Field	13/6/17		Went to New Area & found Dump at another village. Four more lorry loads of stops etc following were dumps in new place.	
	14/6/17		Sent 4 more lorry loads up to New Area & replicated the first days Dump & put them in the new Dump.	
	15/6/17		Moved up to New Area with Divisional HdQrs & cleared all stores shops & new place with Divisional HdQrs & cleared all	
	16/6/17		Collected 4 loads of New stores & sent them forward to our hostels which shall be occupied others in the line.	
	17/6/17		Collected 6 loads of new stores & sent them forward into store. Sent 3 men to Samer.	
	18/6/17		Received 112 bales of Shirt & Socks & sent them up to Coxyde & Dump.	
	19/6/17		Visited Coxyde & found our dump for ships but no place for store. Sent the second Store Tent up & pitches it near the ships as the Reserve Tent.	

1875. Wt. W593/826 1,000,000 4/15 J.B.C. & A. A.D.S.S./Forms/C. 2118.

WAR DIARY
or
INTELLIGENCE SUMMARY
(Erase heading not required.)

Army Form C. 2118

Place	Date	Hour	Summary of Events and Information	Remarks and references to Appendices
In The Field	21/6/17		Busy all day settling in the shops & stores.	
	22/6/17		Visited new A.D.S. at Malo. Les Bains & established the W.O.'s in new tarum refilling points.	
	23/6/17		Received 1 Maltese cart for 1st Dorset - also 62 wheels and 2 Vickers guns, one for 14th and one for 97th M.G. Coy.	
	24/6/17		Received 3 tons Several Stores + 60 wheels. Visited all refilling points & railheads.	
	25/6/17		Received 3 tons Several Stores. Made usual Rounds.	
	26/6/17		Received 10 tons General Stores. Most of it being a dentists store from Base.	
	27/6/17		Dunkerque & suburbs shelled by 15" guns. Very little damage in Dunkerque itself so I went in & local purchase hut found nearly all the shops shut.	
	28/6/17		Received one water cart for A 161 Bde R.F.A.	
	29/6/17		Received 4 tons Several Stores and 2 tons S.D. Clothing also one 6" Newton French Mortar. Visited all dumps & Railhead. Cars visited	

MWS
IV Corps

Army Form C. 2118

WAR DIARY
or
INTELLIGENCE SUMMARY
(Erase heading not required.)

Place	Date	Hour	Summary of Events and Information	Remarks and references to Appendices
In the Field	30/6/17		No stores received from Base. Went to La Panne to deal purchase & visited all Dumps.	

W. Urquhart. Capt.
D.A.D.V.S.
32 Divn.

Confidential	July 1917.

War Diary
of
D.A.D.O.S. 32nd Divn

Volume 2
No 7

WAR DIARY or INTELLIGENCE SUMMARY

Army Form C. 2118

(Erase heading not required.)

Instructions regarding War Diaries and Intelligence Summaries are contained in F.S. Regs., Part II. and the Staff Manual respectively. Title Pages will be prepared in manuscript.

Place	Date	Hour	Summary of Events and Information	Remarks and references to Appendices
In The Field	1/7/17.		Received 10 tons of General Stores from Base. Issued all refilling points. Despatched monthly & Quarterly Returns of Bulk Issues. Prepared account and tons Diary to month of June.	
	2/7/17.		No stores from Base. Issued refilling points & Dunkirk for local Purchase of Torches Electric required for a Special Purpose.	
	3/7/17. 4/7/17.		No stores from Base. Ordinary Routine work. Issued O.C. D.T.C. Received 6 tons General Stores. 49 wheels and H Topics Kitchen Travelling being 2 each for 2" Manchesters and 16 N.F. Also 2 steam Presses being one each to 16 "N.F." & 17 H.L.I. (Proceeded to pts 9 & 96 H.H. Bde to give demonstration of Yukon Packs.	
	5/7/17.		No stores from Base. Issued 10.m. no 3 workshop all refilling points. Ordinary Routine work. H.M the King visited the area today.	
	6/7/17.		Received H tons General stores and 2 tons S.D. Clothing also Motors Spares for 14 Bde M.G. Coy. Issued all refilling points. Druit P.P's was shelled this evening about 7-30 with 8 or 10 shells. No damage done of any sort.	
	7/7/17.		No stores. Issued all refilling points & Cheoles Hideous with W.D.	

Army Form C. 2118

WAR DIARY
or
INTELLIGENCE SUMMARY
(Erase heading not required.)

Instructions regarding War Diaries and Intelligence Summaries are contained in F. S. Regs., Part II. and the Staff Manual respectively. Title Pages will be prepared in manuscript.

Place	Date	Hour	Summary of Events and Information	Remarks and references to Appendices
In The Field.	8/7/17.		Received Bulk Reserves & Horse Shoes. Ordinary Routine work.	
	9/7/17.		Received 370 S. Box Respirators & Horse shoes. Tested all Drums & Shops carried on ordinary Routine work.	
	10/7/17.		No stores up from Base. Proceeded to Dunkirk for local Purchase calling at the A.D.O.S. office on the way to settle matters of difficulty requiring authority to draw 6 Special beds for 6 wd. T.M./Mortars. Artillery fire all day including Bomb f.o. G- all back very heavy. Sent Lorry to D. Army Shops & drew 20 Sponge turning areas, Sent Lorry to rifle Battalion received same 6 .96" & 9" hy Star Rests & 10 rifle Battalion.	
	11/7/17.		Received Bulk General stores and 300 Rifles for Gas shell warnings. Also 4 Telescopic Rifles for 5th Royal Scots in first issue. Also one broken Sun for 219 Mach Gun. Cy. Tested all repairing Drums.	
	12/7/17.		Received 2400 Packs d.G. Magazines and 1200 Braces. Nothing out of ordinary Routine Report.	
	13/7/17		Received Bulk Clothing & Grindery, also 16 Ammunition field for M.G Cyi. from C.M.G.O.	

MM

1875 Wt. W593/826 1,000,000 4/15 J.B.C. & A. A.D.S.S./Forms/C.2118.

WAR DIARY or INTELLIGENCE SUMMARY

Army Form C. 2118

(Erase heading not required.)

Instructions regarding War Diaries and Intelligence Summaries are contained in F.S. Regs., Part II. and the Staff Manual respectively. Title Pages will be prepared in manuscript.

Place	Date	Hour	Summary of Events and Information	Remarks and references to Appendices
In the Field	14/7/17		Received 3 Vickers Guns to 97 M.G. Coy. & 2 Lewis Guns for 15th Lancs Fus. to Class Base to hasten 18pr fuses which had been on demand for a week.	
	15/7/17		Received 2 Vickers Guns from 219 M.G. Coy. Visited Rubbers' Kell refilling points.	
	16/7/17.		Received Bulk Hose shirts & necessaries. Also 11 Lewis Guns for 5th Borders. 1 for 2" KOYLI, 1 for 16" Lancs Fus, 1 for 16" North Fus. & 2 18pr fuses for 2 & 161 Bde R.F.A.	
	17/7/17		Division to be relieved. Went to Trecht area to select store & dump sites. Waited all refilling points.	
	18/7/17		Went in rear of the Reserves & shops drew drumps as no stores sent in. Handed our area stores to 49. Divn Ordnance here up.	
	19/7/17.		Received Bulk Bretton oil & neces also 96 MKII Vickers Barrels with cut attachments & 16 Silvington template M.G. Coys & 2 to water the following guns. 1 Vickers to each of 219 and 14 M.G. Coys: 5 for 97" M.G. Coy. 1 Lewis gun to 1/6 H.L.I. and 2 for 2" Manchesters. 2 Stokes mortars for 97 T.M.B and 1 18pr fuse for 13, 161 Bde R.F.A.	

WAR DIARY
or
INTELLIGENCE SUMMARY

(Erase heading not required.)

Army Form C. 2118

Place	Date	Hour	Summary of Events and Information	Remarks and references to Appendices
In The Field	20/7/17		Received Bulk Clothing from new Railhead. Wrote all the new Refilling points. Sent in draft for DRO to the effect that no Ordnance stores were to be handed in to Lalouze for the future by units. This in order to prevent units dumping stores equipment on Lalouze when about to move. Received 1 18 pr piece only for A.168. 1ste and S.L.G. for 15" H. L. J. + 160 sets Packsaddlery G.S.	
21/7/17.			No stores from Base. No car available. Went my trip. had indent + figures for Bulk love bought in by Lorry.	
22/7/17.			Received Bulk Horse shoes, Nicoanics and 1 18 pr piece for each of A and C 161 1ste R.F.A. and 1 9-45 piece for 1. 32 T.M.B. Visited Refilling points and checked Indents. O.T.	
23/7/17.			No stores from Base. cleared up in store. went a truck of U stores surplus, refls etc to Base. Received 1 u.s. 18 pr carriage for B. 161.	
24/7/17.			No stores. Visited Dumps. Received 1 u.s. 18 pr carriage for B. 161. and 1 carriage 18 pr for B. 161.	
25/7/17.			Received 15 small Tarpaulins General stores and 1400 towell protector nozzle also 1. 2" T.M for Z 32, 1. 18 pr piece for A. 168. 2 carriages 18 pr for A. 168. and 1. 18 pr piece for B. 168. Visited Dump.	

WAR DIARY
or
INTELLIGENCE SUMMARY
(Erase heading not required.)

Army Form C. 2118

Instructions regarding War Diaries and Intelligence Summaries are contained in F. S. Regs., Part II. and the Staff Manual respectively. Title Pages will be prepared in manuscript.

Place	Date	Hour	Summary of Events and Information	Remarks and references to Appendices
In The Field.	26/7/17		No stores up from Base. No Car available.	
	27/7/17		Received Bulk Clothing necessaries. No car so sent a lorry down to bring in Indents. Bulk Figures. Very handicapped owing to lack of car. Consider it an urgent matter that a spare one can be given to each D.A.D.O.S. in lieu of his "mythical" Car.	
	28/7/17		No stores except 1.18p.m piece for B.161. Got car overalls &c dumps.	
	29/7/17		Received Bulk Horse Shoes and 200 Howell Protectors unmade which clears all indents. 1 Lewis gun for 16" drums. Indent all dumps.	
	30/7/17		No store except Water Cart for 7f. M.G. Co. Cleared up store & salvage & clothing & sent off to Base preparatory to move tomorrow. Visited all Dumps.	
	31/7/17		Move postponed. No stores up from Base. Was visited by A.D.O.S XV Corps & D.A.D.O.S 49" who arrange for handing over on Relief. Visited Dumps in a shared car. Wasted a lot of time.	

J Wingerhart. Capt.
D.A.D.O.S 32 Div

Vol 17 Confidential   August 1917.

War Diary
of
DADOS 32ND Division

Volume. 2.
No. 8

Army Form C. 2118

WAR DIARY
or
INTELLIGENCE SUMMARY

(Erase heading not required.)

Instructions regarding War Diaries and Intelligence Summaries are contained in F. S. Regs., Part II. and the Staff Manual respectively. Title Pages will be prepared in manuscript.

Place	Date	Hour	Summary of Events and Information	Remarks and references to Appendices
In The Field.	1/8/17.		Sent up 2 mi lorries with dumps to new area. Received bulk. Several stores. Sent oil & grease. and 1 18pr piece to A. 168. Posted all refilling points.	
	2/8/17.		Distributed stores. Went up more stores & forward area (relays) up ready for move tomorrow.	
	3/8/17.		Moved up & found been occupied forces billets. Brought G.O. of 14" hyd.adv up to him. was refilling points. Visited all dumps & bags(?) to get straight at the central dump.	
	4/8/17		Received 2400 extra water bottles for active operations & a truck of detail stores, including large consignment of deficient parts of the 18 extra 2" T M's received before we left the line. Worked hard all morning at drawing & straightening up the central dump. Visited L.D.G.S. in the afternoon but Col(?) not find him.	
	5/8/17		Visited central dump & all refilling points. No stores up from base. Sent lorry to 15 Corps Troops to collect ammn emergency stores & to take fine barrels &c.	
	6/8/17		Received Bulk Oil & Grease, Sulphur Oil, Grease & Accessories invited dump & W.O.' at Refilling Points.	

MW

Army Form C. 2118

WAR DIARY
or
INTELLIGENCE SUMMARY
(Erase heading not required.)

Instructions regarding War Diaries and Intelligence Summaries are contained in F.S. Regs, Part II. and the Staff Manual respectively. Title Pages will be prepared in manuscript.

Place	Date	Hour	Summary of Events and Information	Remarks and references to Appendices
In The Field.	7/8/17		No letters Received from Base. A.D.V.S. inspected central Dump & divining shafts & had a down from magazine shipped & new shipments in. 32 for design for the information requested by D.A.D.V.S. Col. Thr. Senior Drummer. Obtained permission from the Corps Army to proceed on leave from the 9th to the 19th Aug inclusive.	
	8/8/17.		Made necessary arrangements for going on leave & got the A.D.V.S. to inspect the shops frequently during my absence. Left for Boulogne to catch the Boat on the 9th.	
	20/8/17 9/8/17.		The following stores were received during my absence. Bulk central stores + 32 Rations signal 1½ – for special purpose. Also one 18 pr Gun for C. 161. Bte.	
	11/8/17.		Received 1800 Turn Knots Carrying & Bulk clothing & general stores also 1 Lewis Gun for 16th Lancers. and 1 Mothers Gun for 219 M.G. Cy.	
	12/8/17 13/8/17		Received Bulk Horse shoes & accessories. Bulk General Stores. Also 7 limbered S.S. wagons for D.A.C. Replace 6 U. S.A.A. Carts condemned by S.O.M. Also 1 Lewis Gun for 15th Lancers and 1 for 16th N.F.S.	

MW

WAR DIARY or INTELLIGENCE SUMMARY

Army Form C. 2118

(Erase heading not required.)

Instructions regarding War Diaries and Intelligence Summaries are contained in F.S. Regs., Part II. and the Staff Manual respectively. Title Pages will be prepared in manuscript.

Place	Date	Hour	Summary of Events and Information	Remarks and references to Appendices
In The Field	17/8/17		Received 200 Blankets for Dug outs" & Bulk Clothing Quantity of Pickling Jars. Also 80 Empress Mag. Pocket in lieu of increase of 8 for Watt's Rifle Vickers Gun for 96 in G.H.C.	
	18/8/17		Division withdrawn from the Line with HQrs at La Panne.	
	19/8/17		Received Bulk Horse Chess, necessary arbitrary also 24 Lamps S. Wedges & increased scale & 200 Lights Summons for Klein Junn as send of Magazine. also 1 down Gun for 16" Lines. Returned from leave late at night. Took charge again. Unrented Groups & all repelling parties reported not Satisfactory	
	20/8/17		Went Round all dumps & repelling points.	
	21/8/17		J.C. hom Stanley from 96 Inf Bde to Chief Clerk of 66 Div in exchange one S.C. Johnson from 66 Div. Received Balance of the Compasses Mag. Pocket.	
	22/8/17		Received Bulk Equipment, several stores & rested D.A.D.O.S. 66 Div. & all repelling Points centred through in the afternoon. Went to Dunkirk in the morning for local Purchase. Also received 1.18 pm Gun for C.168 Bde.	
	23/8/17		No done, from Bere. Visited Dumps & Repelling points- Road leading to Oluny Shelter heavily seen after Sept.	

Army Form C. 2118

'WAR DIARY
or
INTELLIGENCE SUMMARY

(Erase heading not required.)

Instructions regarding War Diaries and Intelligence
Summaries are contained in F. S. Regs., Part II.
and the Staff Manual respectively. Title Pages
will be prepared in manuscript.

Place	Date	Hour	Summary of Events and Information	Remarks and references to Appendices
In the Field	24/8/17		Received Bulk Clothing & Sundry Stores. Stables have to clean up one or two matters. Visited 96th Inf. Bde on my way back.	
	25/8/17		Received 500 tins water carrying, visited dumps of 96th & 97th Bdes & writing points & saw Staff Captains of these Brigades.	
	26/8/17		Received Bulk Horse Shoes, receiving a further 100 Blankets for Div arty. Went into Dunkirk for local purchase & called on A.D.S.T. on return journey. Visited Central Dump & 14th Bde dump in the afternoon.	
	27/8/17		No stores received from Base. Spent the whole day in the office except visiting the 14th Bde dump.	
	28/8/17		Visited A.D.O.S. Corps, 96th Inf. Bde Central Dump & all refilling points selecting new sites for the latter as the old ones had been "found" by enemy shells.	
	29/8/17		Moved back to old billets in Argyle. Refilling points are in practically the same place. Central dump has not moved. Received 6 tons of general stores. Visited Central Dump & refilling points. Enemy shelling Crayde area about noon with about 2 dozen H.E. 15 c.m. and. [sig]	

WAR DIARY
or
INTELLIGENCE SUMMARY

(Erase heading not required.)

Army Form C. 2118

Place	Date	Hour	Summary of Events and Information	Remarks and references to Appendices
In The Field	30/8/17		Received 6 tons of General Stores and one broken lorry for 219 M.G.C. Central Dump was heavily shelled with 5.9 H.V. & refilling points also. Visited all these places & decided to run Central Dump & ships up here near the office. Do that if only five closer supervision in times of trouble. Moved up the Store Tent in the evening. Ships will follow next day.	
	31/8/17		Received 5 tons of Clothing, Sundries & boots &c. Got all ships (Central Dump established) near my office as a result of moving Shelling. Spent all day in the offices setting out schemes to be handed tonight etc. & superintending the erection of the Tent &c.	

Marshall Capt.
A.A.D.S.
N.R.D.S.
32 Div.

31/8/17

Vol 18

War Diary
of
D.A.D.O.S. 32ND DIVN

VOLUME   2
No.   9

Army Form C. 2118

WAR DIARY
or
INTELLIGENCE SUMMARY
(Erase heading not required.)

Instructions regarding War Diaries and Intelligence Summaries are contained in F. S. Regs., Part II. and the Staff Manual respectively. Title Pages will be prepared in manuscript.

Place	Date	Hour	Summary of Events and Information	Remarks and references to Appendices
In The Field.	1/9/17		No stores from Base. Visited refilling point & proceeded to Dunkirk for local Purchase.	
	2/9/17.		Received Bulk Clothing and Saddlery. Was visited by D.D.O.S. of "Army". A.D.O.S. XV Corps who inspected Shops & Central Dump.	
	3/9/17.		Received from Bulk Horse Shoes & necessaries. Visited all refilling & examined all outstanding indent - to see if they had been checked with unit representatives. Found all satisfactory.	
	4/9/17.		Proceeded to Heavy Mobile shop to take various article for Repair after visiting refilling point. Went on to Dunkirk for local Purchase returned at 12-30. No stores from Base.	
	5/9/17.		Refilling points were heavily shelled during the afternoon & S.C. Ruswell was dangerously wounded. The enemy shell this area daily & so decided to bring all W.T. to a central dump near the office. Proceeded to Dunkirk in the morning for local Purchase of Heavy Metals Shop. Received Bulk Picketing Gear, Dubbin oil & grease.	
	6/9/17.		No stores from Base. Moved all the W.T. up to New dump. Notified Units of the Change.	

MMK

Army Form C. 2118

WAR DIARY
or
INTELLIGENCE SUMMARY
(Erase heading not required.)

Instructions regarding War Diaries and Intelligence Summaries are contained in F. S. Regs., Part II. and the Staff Manual respectively. Title Pages will be prepared in manuscript.

Place	Date	Hour	Summary of Events and Information	Remarks and references to Appendices
In the Field	7/9/17		Received 4 Truck of Blankets, 1 Truck of Gds /21 & replace Horses) 1 Truck of S.D. Clothing & Boots. Sundry villate necessaries.	
	8/9/17		14 stores from Base. Proceeded to Dunkirk for local Purchase wealk at heavy shop to collect repaired Compasses & Binoculars.	
	9/9/17		No stores from Base. Erected Store Tent at central Dump & camouflaged it. Ordinary Routine work.	
	10/9/17		S.C. Lancaster repd. to duty in place of S.C. Russell (wounded) & evacuated. Received Bulk Stores/Stores necessaries. 2 Lewis Guns for 1st Dorset Regt. 24 Superscopes & 26 Runners Signalling increase of 2 pr Batt. & 64 A.A. sights for Vickers Guns Infantry Report.	
	11/9/17		Received one Inf part began Dunkd G.S. to 10" M.G.C.	
	12/9/17		Received Bulk Ration. Oil. Grease & general stores. also 200 Blankets for bag oils, 4 shower Horns etc. S.C. King went sick. Visited by R.D.O.S. who inspected shops etc.	
	13/9/17		No stores from Base. Visited Dunkirk for Local Purchase oakum & Army Heavy Shops.	
	14/9/17		Received one Carts officers mess fur 200 7? Cy Rt & Sundry Clothing. Grindery. Boot & State necessaries.	

WAR DIARY
or
INTELLIGENCE SUMMARY
(Erase heading not required.)

Army Form C. 2118

Place	Date	Hour	Summary of Events and Information	Remarks and references to Appendices
In The Field	15/9/17		No stores from Base. Visited 14" Bde H.Q". & A.D.O.S. The bullets were not the front H.Q. recently shelled by enemy from 7 p.m. to 10 p.m. & at intervals during the night.	
	16/9/17		Received Bath House shoes. Receiving also 60 each of No's 22 & 20 Grenade survey to Practice trenches.	
	17/9/17		Received no forge G.S. for 32 - B.A.C. and no Carriage 16 pr for C. 168 Bde R.F.A.	
	18/9/17		Went to Corps to take over from A.D.O.S. who goes on leave today. Went through papers etc. & arranged to go on each afternoon to stay as long as required.	
	19/9/17		Received Bath button Oil. Lamp Spares Picketing Gear also 13 left Range firing templates, increased scale of Brome forms 2 & 3 for Battns. Went to A.D.O.S. office in the afternoon - dealt with papers. Nothing of any particular importance came from XV Corps & 9 Bat Brown machine Gun from XV Corps.	
	20/9/17		No stores up from Base. Went to Corps & did the necessary office work & took some important papers to Q. Called on O.O. XV Corps Troops from a light Railway switch not progressing very fast.	

WAR DIARY
or
INTELLIGENCE SUMMARY

(Erase heading not required.)

Army Form C. 2118

Place	Date	Hour	Summary of Events and Information	Remarks and references to Appendices
In the Field	21/9/17		Received Bulk Clothing, Sundry Stable necessaries also Box Respirators & 1 mess cart for each of 218 & 219 Field Coys R.E. and 2 kitchen guns for 14th M.G. Coy. Went to Dieppe in the afternoon & did the usual office work & hastened the completion of light Railway from Blanket store to Road.	
	22/9/17		No stores from Base. Boot & Heavy Mobile Shops & Corps H.Qrs. performed the usual Routine work.	
	23/9/17		(Received) Bulk Horse Shoes & 13 modified packs to Lewis Guns; went to Drancheim for bread purchase & 8 Corps H.Qrs. Nothing out of the ordinary to report.	
	24/9/17		No stores from Base. Went to Heavy Mobile Shops, collected Binoculars etc & on to Corps for usual Routine work.	
	25/9/17		No stores from Base. Visited 16th D.A.D.O.S. to Corps. Saw D.A.D.O.S. 42 Bn. & 16 M.G. Barrel. The property of the Corps. Saw D.A.D.O.S. 42 Bn. & did Routine work at Corps H.Qrs.	
	26/9/17		Went to Heavy Mobile Shop & collected 15 kitchen tripods, 8 N.A. Lamps & delivered 6 to Corps Troops. Received A.A. Guns & 80 sights N.A. Lamps etc. to mountings 8 two General Stores & 6 Trucks of Pontoon Stores from 218 & 219 F.Coy R.E. and 1 kitchen Gun for 16th M.G.C. & 1 Limber for 2-mules-draught. Ordinary Routine work at Corps. HW.	

Army Form C. 2118

WAR DIARY
or
INTELLIGENCE SUMMARY
(Erase heading not required.)

Instructions regarding War Diaries and Intelligence Summaries are contained in F. S. Regs., Part II. and the Staff Manual respectively. Title Pages will be prepared in manuscript.

Place	Date	Hour	Summary of Events and Information	Remarks and references to Appendices
In the Field.	27/9/17.		Received 3 Trucks of Pontoon Stores for 218 + 219 3rd Coy R.E. Went to tps. & arranged for fatigue Party & 1000 Blankets for next day - ended ordinary Routine work.	
	28/9/17.		Received 2 Trains of Several stores and 5 tons clothing. Collected 6000 Blankets & took 1000 Blankets to Poperinghe for disinfection. Was in bed all day. Sent 400 Gn shelter all thro' the evening night. Chief Clerk of A.D.O.S. Corps brought me the routine papers to sign.	
	29/9/17.		No stores from Base. Was at H broad Corps & do the usual Routine work.	
	30/9/17.		Received Buck Horse Shoes & Necessaries from Base. Visited 41st + 42nd D.A.D's O.S. & cleared up all papers at the Corps ready for the A.D.O.S. return tonight. Nothing unusual to report.	

30/9/17.

Murquhart Capt.
D.A.D.O.S. 32nd Divn.

WAR DIARY
OF
D.A.D.O.S. 32 Divn.
For October 1917

Army Form C. 2118

WAR DIARY
or
INTELLIGENCE SUMMARY
(Erase heading not required.)

Instructions regarding War Diaries and Intelligence Summaries are contained in F. S. Regs., Part II. and the Staff Manual respectively. Title Pages will be prepared in manuscript.

Place	Date	Hour	Summary of Events and Information	Remarks and references to Appendices
In the Field	1/10/17		No stores from Base. Was visited by D.A.D.O.S 42" Div whom I showed round as they were supposed to be taking over from us. Nothing out of the ordinary routine to report.	
	2/10/17		No stores from Base. Visited A.D.O.S. II Corps and no 34.19 Advance mobile workshop, and Duncerque for local purchase.	
	3/10/17		Received Bath Equipment, Picketing gear, oil grease and also 1 Lewis Gun to 96 Royal Scots. Visited D.A.D.O.S. 41st Div.	
	4/10/17		No stores from Base. Called on Packsaddley + Corps mule cutter, etc. preparatory to handing over Entrenching Division.	
	5/10/17		Received Bath Clothing, Grindery, Saddlery staff necessaries. We are to be relieved by 42" Div 1st October. 42" which makes handing over difficult. Saw both D.A.D.O.S. + made all necessary arrangements.	
	6/10/17		No stores from Base. Busy all day sorting + listing stores to be handed over to Entrenching some down to Corps store for storage.	
	7/10/17		Fixed with Divnl H.Q. re La Panne. Inclemently wet day. Visited 14 Inf Bde + 76 Inf Bde H.Q. Gun.	
	8/10/17		No stores from Base.	
	9/10/17		No store from Base. Nothing to report.	

W.W.

Army Form C. 2118

WAR DIARY
or
INTELLIGENCE SUMMARY
(Erase heading not required.)

Instructions regarding War Diaries and Intelligence Summaries are contained in F. S. Regs., Part II. and the Staff Manual respectively. Title Pages will be prepared in manuscript.

Place	Date	Hour	Summary of Events and Information	Remarks and references to Appendices
In the Field	10/10/17		No stores from base. Division moving to Roesdael. Went to Billeting. Not very satisfactory accommodation for stores. Put can manage.	
	11/10/17		Moved to Roesdael. Received stores from base.	
	12/10/17		Visited all three Brigades & 499 Gns of 161 & 166 Artillery Brigades. Received full allotment of 20 steinall stone clippers. Also full trenches, respirator, nil Grease stone Respirator. Visited 96" Inf Bde & 15 Divn & 16 N.Z. all well.	
	14/10/17.		No stores from base. Visited 14" Inf Bde & 96 Royal Scots. No complaints.	
	15/10/17.		Proceeded to Calais to hasten various items.	
	16/10/17		Received Bath Staple necessarys and 12 Telescopic Rifles to complete Battalion to 5 per Battn. Some Artillery Group left us.	
	17/10/17		Visited 97" Inf Bde & Heavy trestle shops	
	18/10/17		Received Bath clothing, horse shoes & necessaries. Visited A.D.V.S. & 96" Inf Bde.	

[signature]

Army Form C. 2118.

WAR DIARY
or
INTELLIGENCE SUMMARY

(Erase heading not required.)

Instructions regarding War Diaries and Intelligence Summaries are contained in F. S. Regs., Part II. and the Staff Manual respectively. Title Pages will be prepared in manuscript.

Place	Date	Hour	Summary of Events and Information	Remarks and references to Appendices
In The Field.	19/10/17		No stores from Base. Proceeded to Calais to hasten home Rugs & arranged to send a lorry to collect 500 tomorrow.	
	20/10/17		Received Bath Drawers, Equipment, oil sheets, ricketing gear. Sent lorry to rendezvous for Home Rugs.	
	21/10/17		Men will have to move to "Hush" Camp as Lorry went to come into an 'isilet' wing to being bombed. Not much to choose between the 2 places. Loving the 500 Home Rugs.	
	22/10/17		Received Bath Clothing etc & issued it to Bdes. same day as we have to move tomorrow.	
	23/10/17		Moved to "Hush" Camp. Beastly Hole. No accommodation for anything. Had to pitch a store Tent. S.Mr.T.O. bungled order for lorries & move was not finished till very late. Rained all morning.	
	24/10/17		Proceeded to Bray Dunes to see A.D.O.S. & owing he had been sent to Hospital, locum in there but could not see him. Sent Mc Hood to G.H.Q. in trial for post of Sergeant Clerk.	
	25/10/17		Proceeded to New Tree to see about Billet. No accommodation for all my personnel (Finis) up store at Atwide & Shops offices at Dnid Sd D---- St ledger 2000. W.O. not at Brigades. MW	

2449 Wt. W14957/Mgo 750,000 1/16 J.B.C. & A. Forms/C.2118/12.

WAR DIARY or INTELLIGENCE SUMMARY

Army Form C. 2118.

(Erase heading not required.)

Place	Date	Hour	Summary of Events and Information	Remarks and references to Appendices
In The Field.	26/10/17		Moved from "Knot" Camp to Edersele. Established central dump & 4th Bde Dump in good buildings near Proven Railhead. 97th Bde Dump at Rubrouck & 96th Bde Dump at Eringhem. Shops did not arrive till 9.30 p.m.	
	27/10/17		Visited Railhead. No stores up from Base. Visited Staff Captains of all three Brigades & saw several Quartermasters.	
	28/10/17		Received 2 trucks of Vests woollen & Complete to per man limits scale & sent same to Brigades. Wired my representative with 50th Divn to draw the Artillery allotment. Visited all three Brigades.	
	29/10/17		No stores up from Base so visited Calais & procured 5000 yds. of Tape for Farriery purposes & hastened delivery of Leather Jerkins.	
	30/10/17		Received Bulk clothing necessaries & horse shoes rivetted all three Brigade Staff Captains & my own dumps. Proceeded to Kent Kerk & procured lorry to deliver 1200 dummy cartridges.	
	31/10/17		Received Body bands from Base & issued them & proceeded to all three Brigades & dumps.	

MWurquhart Capt.
D.A.D.O.S. 32nd Div.

WAR DIARY or INTELLIGENCE SUMMARY

Army Form C. 2118.

DADOS 32 Vol 20

Place	Date	Hour	Summary of Events and Information	Remarks and references to Appendices
In the Field	1/11/17		Proceeded to D.A.D.O.S. 58 Div. as it is understood we are to relieve that Divn & went on to Abramed Dune A.S. Q⁵ on Canal Bank. Proceeded to Railhead & Central Dump in the afternoon. Received Bulk Knapsacks & Haversacks.	
	2/11/17.		Visited Railhead Central Dump & all three Brigades in the morning. No stores from Base. Proceeded to D/men in the afternoon to locate purchases.	
	3/11/17.		Received Equip, went & picketing gear & called at Railhead & all three Brigades. Also called on AD O S II Corps. Received 1450 Rugs since Brigades.	
	4/11/17		Received 2ⁿᵈ Blanket per man 11,500 to complete, sent them straight out to Brigades, delivered direct to Units where possible. Visited all Brigades & Staff Captains.	
	5/11/17		No stores from Base. Visited Dump twice & sent out lorry load of stores for them.	
	6/11/17.		Received 1 ton General Stores from Base. Visited Railhead & all three Brigades.	
	7/11/17.		No stores from Base. Went to Pperinghe to see DADOS 63ʳᵈ Div who we are supposed to relieve. Arranged to take over Dump offices.	

Army Form C. 2118.

WAR DIARY
or
INTELLIGENCE SUMMARY
(Erase heading not required.)

Instructions regarding War Diaries and Intelligence Summaries are contained in F.S. Regs., Part II. and the Staff Manual respectively. Title Pages will be prepared in manuscript.

Place	Date	Hour	Summary of Events and Information	Remarks and references to Appendices
In The Field	8/10/17.		No stores from Base. Proceeded to all refilling points & Brigades in the morning & to St Omer in the afternoon for local purchase.	
	9/10/17.		Received Cap'n Necessaries & Horse shoes & also allotment of Field Service Boots. Suspended lorries from Base in view of Monday the 11th.	
	10/10/17.		Visited all Brigades & arranged for Collection of W.O.'s & any stores they had left for the morning, arranged for 5 extra lorries for the move.	
	11/10/17.		Moved up to Noyrenghe & completed move in good time, got a good billet for the officers. Everyone satisfied except the W.O. who have not too much room. Must write to Divt 3 class Advance men & Horse Base for Infantry & two useless P.B. men sent to replace them.	
	12/10/17.		Adopted the central Dump scheme as accomodation not available at Belts a refilling points. Visited 97 Inf Bde Staff Captain.	
	13/10/17.		Visited Railhead. No stores. Proceeded to see ADOS E Caps. + Supply Dumps.	
	14/10/17.		Received Bulk Ordnance Stores, LD Clothing & Saddlery. Visited Railhead & 97 Inf Bde.	
	15/10/17.		Received 4 tons General Stores & visited Railhead & 96 Inf Bde & More Hooper Collins.	MW

Army Form C. 2118.

WAR DIARY
or
INTELLIGENCE SUMMARY
(Erase heading not required.)

Place	Date	Hour	Summary of Events and Information	Remarks and references to Appendices
In the Field	16/10/17		Received stable necessaries, S.D. Clothing, Boot Ankle, Lamp, oil & grease, & stable necessaries. Visited all sides of gun.	
	17/10/17		Received equipment sundry but no leather & stable necessaries. Visited sections HQ Gn + SA Bys S8 to see my representative arrangements for their return to line.	
	18/10/17		Received more sundry but again no leather. Proceeded to 66" Bn & obtained 10 setts of leather which helped considerably. Visited Corps Salvage Dumps & obtained packs. Got 40. Visited 76" Inf Bde & Sdrs to Gn to arrange no stores from Base when necessary for taking over.	
	19/10/17		No stores from Base. Went to Calais HQy & obtain various stores urgently required before going into the line. Received 4000 Bags Rifle Covers from Calais. SDGS having sent special chap to collect same.	
	20/10/17		No stores from Base. Visited Railhead & got 60 packs urgently required. Visited 66 Gn again & got some surplus pouches magazine L.G.	
	21/10/17		Received small quantity of general stores & 533 Jerkins leather. Nothing to report.	
	22/10/17			

MW.

WAR DIARY or INTELLIGENCE SUMMARY

Army Form C. 2118.

Place	Date	Hour	Summary of Events and Information	Remarks and references to Appendices
In the Field	23/10/17		No stores from Base. Visited 1st Divn. Sent up & erected store tent in their dump for the move next day.	
	24/10/17		Moved up to Brake Camp & sent lorries on to Ruickeard to collect bulk S.D. Clothing, stable necessaries & equipment. Any stores lay.	
	25/10/17		Visited Advanced D.H.Q. at Canal Bank & shops which have had to be left in Poperinghe owing to lack of accommodation. No stores. Received Caps, necessaries Sunday with 98 tent leather. Visited D.H.Q.	
	26/10/17		& shops in Poperinghe & Ruickeard. Attended conference of D.A.D's with A.D.O.S. Friching & on return. Received bulk stove shoes, necessaries & 500 blankets to complete to scale. Visited shops & B.H.Q.	
	27/10/17		No stores from Base. Visited C.R.A. & attended conference on the rendering of return of guns etc. Rendered the return required & so far no criticism has arisen.	
	28/10/17		Received Belts, Buttons, oil & necessaries & necessaries. Visited shops & D.H.Q.	
	29/10/17		Received S.D. Clothing Sundry & proceeded after visiting D.H.Q. to St. Omer for urgent local purchase.	
	30/10/17			

Murquhart. Capt.
D.A.D.O.S. 32 Divn.

WAR DIARY
for the month of
December 1917
D.A.D.O.S. 32nd Division

Army Form C. 2118.

WAR DIARY
INTELLIGENCE SUMMARY

(Erase heading not required.)

Instructions regarding War Diaries and Intelligence Summaries are contained in F. S. Regs., Part II. and the Staff Manual respectively. Title Pages will be prepared in manuscript.

Place	Date	Hour	Summary of Events and Information	Remarks and references to Appendices
In The Field	1/12/17		No stores from Base. Rested. Advanced H.Q.rs in the morning + also Chops. Sent off August Acct. War Diary + Return of Bulk Stores. Received phone 1 Vickers Gun + 2 Tripod mountings to 97th M.G.C.	
	2/12/17.		3 Trucks of stores up + one lorry detailed to deliver Trench Shelters to Frost Farm. Visited D.A.D.O.S. of 35 + 63 Divn. & Hq + borrow a lorry to help after applying without avail to Corps, locat. & am supply Column + got one. Had to send one other lorry to Centre for Water Bottles. Issued 3 Lewis Guns + 2 Bipod mountings + 2 Knuckletings. Received 2 Vickers + 2 Tripod mountings for 14 M.G.C. Collected 6 Bipod mountings from Salvage.	
	3/12/17.		Drew 200 Brassoes from II Corps & distributed according to Pirekmont. Visited D.A.D.O.S II Corps + Advanced D.H.Q. in the morning then the afternoon went to Coulture & look for accumulation when we are relieved.	
	5/12/17 to 9/12/17		A total of 31 Tons of Genl Stores was received from the Base	
	11-12-17		The Advce Dump was moved from Private Camp to Sheet 28 A 23 A 5 0 together with Ammunon + Divisional Stores who were at Poperinghe. Thus making the Divisional Advanced Supply Centre. Moved to 5 Camp. St Sixtus Soyen - Proverbs Road. Toto Mording	
	12.12.17		+ Trucks arrived were handed over. Camelles not for use of French Dek.	

Army Form C. 2118.

WAR DIARY
or
INTELLIGENCE SUMMARY
(Erase heading not required.)

Instructions regarding War Diaries and Intelligence Summaries are contained in F.S. Regs., Part II. and the Staff Manual respectively. Title Pages will be prepared in manuscript.

Place	Date	Hour	Summary of Events and Information	Remarks and references to Appendices
Havre	12/12/17		Capt. V.W. Urquhart granted leave to England from 14th to 13th January 1918	
	14/12/17		7 Tons of Stores & Clothing received - 378 sets of Surplus Packsaddlery sent to Railhead for despatch to Base.	
	15/12/17		Hands on Cash in Hand and Imprest Acct to Capt. Robertson Arny Canteen Officer who was appointed Purchasing Officer during the absence of the O.M.O.S. 7 Tons of General Stores also received	
	16/12/17		Lorries sent to Brake Camp to fetch 2 Tarpaulin Huts for erection in Rest Camp. As the conditions under which Tailors & Shoemakers these accommodated namely Tents, were unsuitable for them to satisfactorily carry out their work. 10 Tons of General Stores & 80x Horseshoes were drawn from Railhead Pte Lakes Polyhothoe (Class B man) posted for duty with O.M.O.S Staff	
	17/12/17		Lorries Cap Waterproof for requirements of Division arrived, these however were not issued in view of S.R.O. 12951. 14 Tons of Rent Stores were also received.	
	18/12/17		Pte Robert H. Grahams and Pte E. Riddell 1st Cameron (P.B men on Probation) for transfer to R.O.C.) returned to Base. Being quite unsuitable	
	19/12/17		Surplus Yukon Packs - Water Carriers - Pack Cradles Carriers & a small quantity of Packsaddlery returned to Base under instructions of Corps (These stores having been left behind by the Divisions in Dungeons) a further issue of Towels & Tub Washing was made to Corps Camp for Trench feet.	
	20/12/17		150 Swingtrees manufactured in Army Shops from Park & Beam Trees delivered to Divisional AOpal the Reserve for 1.P. Lewis Guns was returned to Gun Park.	

249 Wt. W4957/M99. 750,000 1/16 J.B.C. &A. Forms/C.2118/12.

Army Form C. 2118.

WAR DIARY
INTELLIGENCE SUMMARY
(Erase heading not required.)

Instructions regarding War Diaries and Intelligence Summaries are contained in F. S. Regs., Part II. and the Staff Manual respectively. Title Pages will be prepared in manuscript.

Place	Date	Hour	Summary of Events and Information	Remarks and references to Appendices
S.R. Depot	21/12/17		6 Tons of Tent Stores & 93 Cases of Anti-Gas Stores received from Base. The Detachment was paid by Capt Robertson. Sapper Stores were urgently reqd for trench feet - none were available at Corps Troops. Base promised by wire to urge delivery of same. 3 Stores Sapper dues in Indent 32/5391 of 30th received.	
	23/12/17		7 Tons of Stores received.	
	24/12/17		Tons of Tent Stores received.	
	25/12/17		Reported to NABQMG with reference to handing over of additional Battle Stores received to Division etc.	
	28/12/17		8 Tons of Tent Stores received which included 6 Sapper Stores. Application made for additional 6 Lorries to move Stores into new Area.	
	29/12/17			
	30/12/17		10 Lorries & 1 Order Stores with Personnel moved to Zuidschote. The Order Dumps allotted for the Stores was much too small & Office unsuitable. Short long procured. Moved Office into new Billet - and arranged in Conjunction with Bellburg Officer & OC RE Employment Co to exchange trams allotted for sleeping apartments of labours Employment men for the tram allotted to NABQMG for Stores. The Billeting Officer also arranged that Offices would be exchanged on the 1st Jan. The latter Order was afterwards cancelled.	
	31/12/17		4 Lorries kept to be sent back to Clean Dump at Brake Camp - all returned by 11 pm. The NCO i/c was left at Brake Camp reported that all stores were clear.	

for D.A.D.O.S. 323 Div[?]

WAR DIARY or INTELLIGENCE SUMMARY

Army Form C. 2118.

Place	Date	Hour	Summary of Events and Information	Remarks and references to Appendices
In the field	1/1/18		Moved Office into new billet. Also Pole Dumps & Reserve stores into Barn previously occupied by Employment & Salvage men.	
	2/1/18		7 Tons of Genl Stores. 4 Hand Carts received.	
	3/1/18		1 K.T. & 22 Wheels received. Arranged with Staff Capt 96th Inf Bde that Ordce Stores would be delivered at Licques for Units of that Bde on certain days which would be arranged as circumstances arose owing to distance Units were situated from Main Dumps. 1 Lorry with Ordce stores for Artillery Units sent to DAC HQrs.	
	4/1/18		7 Tons of Genl Stores received. 1 Lorry containing stores for Units of 96th Bde sent to Licques.	
	5/1/18		1 Lorry sent to DAC HQrs with stores for Arnt Artillery Units, also 1 Lorry sent to Ordce Depôt Calais to ret. some Front Corps. supplies which were urgently reqd by Units. Trenches Tape & Nails was obtained. Left only a small supply of ½" Front Corps obtained. The Base informs Ordce Representatives that supplies were sent from home had been practically received.	
	6/1/18		5 Tons of Genl Stores which included Chiefly Horse Shoes and a further Small Supply of 3/8" Front Corps - a proportion of Front Corps was issued to all Units.	
	7/1/18		1 Ton of Stores - Chiefly Oats, Shepherds Knives received. As more of Amt Artillery was brought forward it was arranged with Officer that they would be transferred to 39th Dm. Lorry with Lt. V. Stevenson with Artillery stores was sent to forward area to DAHQs 39 Div for the purpose of administering Artillery. Arranged with Area Comdt for the use of a farmhouse near Wattou (which is Amt Railhead) as a Department in the event of Hqs setting in a Barn (Pichet (91) was ambulated at such times y regt. The Barn is situated about ½ a Kilo from Railhead. There was no suitable place to erect a Store Tent which in the first place was the intention.	

WAR DIARY
or
INTELLIGENCE SUMMARY

(Erase heading not required.)

Army Form C. 2118.

Place	Date	Hour	Summary of Events and Information	Remarks and references to Appendices
8/1/18	In the field		Lorry sent to 96th Bde H.Qrs with stores. Arranged with Q that all Battalions should return machine guns to Bde Armourer's Shop for periodical repairs. Sent Lorry to St Omer and purchased a Sewing Machine for use in Tailor's Shop for the repair of 1/170 Frames. The Lorry sent to Lieques got ditched. Lorry with Sgt Hammersman from forward area returned.	
In the field	9.1.18		6 Tons of Genl Stores received. 96th Bde Lorry returned. Transferred 17 N.Z. P.L. 85th F.A. Bn.	
— do —	10.1.18		1 Lorry sent to St Omer, w stores sent to SAA&B 39 R.Br. to administer Artillery.	
— do —	11.1.18		2 Tons Genl Stores received. 1 Lorry sent to 96th Bde with stores. 2nd M.O.V.L. 1 Transports to 35th May Hn.	
— do —	12.1.18		Thaw precautions adopted from 11 AM. Sent representative to Railhead to clean Train, and to arrange the loading men of Billet 196. Arranged with "Q" for 6 Waggons to be detailed to be at Railhead morning of 13th inst to move stores.	
— do —	13.1.18		6 G.S Waggons sent to Railhead to clear 95.00 Tons Stores. 1 Major with stores sent to Wizernes. Captn Urquhart returns off leave.	
	14-1-18		4 inches snow fell in the night. No stores up from base. Spent the day in office & stores	
	15-1-18		No stores from base hoisted 96 & 97 Bde to Q. Thaw precautions still in force.	
	16-1-18		No stores from base. Proceeded to Calais to obtain some first logs in view of approaching move back of the line. No logs available but got 2 cwt of shoe nails. Arranged for 4 lorries to be detailed transport in the week.	
	17/-1-18		Received Saddlery Oil, Grease Equipment horse shoe nails clothing 2 early horse transport had to leave part of the stores at Railhead Dump.	MU.

2449 Wt. W14957/M90 750,000 1/16 J.B.C. & A. Forms/C.2118/12.

Army Form C. 2118.

WAR DIARY
or
INTELLIGENCE SUMMARY

(Erase heading not required.)

Place	Date	Hour	Summary of Events and Information	Remarks and references to Appendices
In the Field	18/1/18.		Move definitely arranged & no Brigade starts tomorrow. Suspended leave from Base. Arranged for a store in Poperinghe as our present will not be vacant till 29th inst.	
	19/1/18.		Sent 7 lorry loads of stores in to Poperinghe Store with order to stay overnight & return next day. Sent one lorry to Railhead with salvage.	
	20/1/18.		Cleared two lorries of salvage to Railhead. All lorries arrived safely & 6 were loaded for next day's trip. One going in to Poperinghe to return tomorrow so as to take office up on 22nd inst with the rest of Divl. H.Q.	
	21/1/18.		Sent off 6 lorries with all remaining stores, workshop, etc, my personal office kitstuff left. Lorry reported back safely. (Received) wire from W.O. notifying safe arrival at Poperinghe.	
	22/1/18.		Moved with Divl. H.Q. up to Road's Camp & was allotted a car for my own use whilst attached to Advanced D.H.Q.	
	23/1/18.		Visited Dump at Poperinghe & received Bulk Issue Stores Orderly Cpl. Press, both mobile equipment & Picketing for Mules arranged D.H.Q. at Canal Bank.	
	24/1/18.		Sent Tailor & Armourer Shop & Bath Tailor shop to an old dump on Klimendern Road, to hold the Dump till we could get to other stores move up. Visited H.Q. at Canal Bank.	

W.W.

2449 Wt. W14957/Mgo 750,000 1/16 J.B.C. & A. Forms/C.2118/12.

WAR DIARY
INTELLIGENCE SUMMARY

Army Form C. 2118.

Place	Date	Hour	Summary of Events and Information	Remarks and references to Appendices
In The Field.	25/1/18		Visited H.Q. Qr. 14 "Inf. Bde." & H.Q. Qr. 18" Divn. with view to inspecting new site they were building for their Ordnance Dump. Found it unsuitable. Went on to Canal Bank & got authority from Q. to have a store shed & ammunition dump erected. Have built & got an indent from C.R.E. to draw the necessary material. Visited D.A.D.O.S. I Divn & took over his Dump too.	
	26/1/18		Received Bulk Clothing, Ironmongery, Necessaries & Boots ankle. Went to Calais. Busy to clear up several matters on Indents etc.	
	27/1/18		Received further Bulk S.D. Clothing & managed to stop Bulk demand from going until amended. Very difficult nowadays to deal with Calais as no attention is paid to me, not "In charge" last week Both in Advice & we have many duplicate issues which tend to make rearranging issues. Visited Canal Bank & got the loan of two sappers to assist in building the Dump.	
	28/1/18		Obtained material from Dumps & sent S/Sgt Elkin & four men to revisit sappers & commence erection. Visited O.O.T. Capt Trotter & completed move up to Everlinghe Road Dump.	
	29/1/18		Visited D.A.D.O.S. 18" Divn. & arranged to taking over various stores & went on to Canal Bank.	

Army Form C. 2118.

WAR DIARY
or
INTELLIGENCE SUMMARY
(Erase heading not required.)

Instructions regarding War Diaries and Intelligence Summaries are contained in F. S. Regs., Part II. and the Staff Manual respectively. Title Pages will be prepared in manuscript.

Place	Date	Hour	Summary of Events and Information	Remarks and references to Appendices
In the Field	30/1/18		Moved office up to Welsh Farm with D.H.Q. Moved W.O.'s reasonable kits up to new Dump at Elverdinghe Chateau. Store shed finished. Armourers shop begun. Received Accessories, Equipment, Dubbin and Grease from Base.	
	31/1/18.		Sent to Army Sniping School took two rifles for repair through Base Park in exchange. Moved reserve stores up to new Dump. No stores up from Base.	

M. Urquhart Capt.
S.A.O.T.S.
32. Div.

Confidential   February 1918.

9623

War Diary

of

D.A.D.O.S.

32nd Division.

VOLUME _____ No. _____

Army Form C. 2118.

WAR DIARY
or
INTELLIGENCE SUMMARY
(Erase heading not required.)

Instructions regarding War Diaries and Intelligence Summaries are contained in F. S. Regs., Part II. and the Staff Manual respectively. Title Pages will be prepared in manuscript.

Place	Date	Hour	Summary of Events and Information	Remarks and references to Appendices
In the Field	1/2/18		Rec'd Bulk Clothing, Boots, Stable necessaries, and 45 Pistols. Visited Railhead and 14th Bde. & 9th.	
	2/2/18		No stores up from Base. Visited Enbarge Dump at Hanescarpe Poperinghe and Khondanghe.	
	3/2/18		Rec'd Bulk Sunday necessaries. Home shoes & a further 20 Pistols. 3000 shirts to stock for Divnl. Baths & 8 layers stores to Divnl. Rest Station. Visited Divnl. Rest Station & A.D.O.S. 2nd Corps.	
	4/2/18		Proceeded to Calais to settle various questions. Very cold drive & a succession of punctures. Unable to all the way back. No stores up from Base.	
	5/2/18		In stores. Nothing urgent but various Routine work.	
	6/2/18		Rec'd Bulk Butter, oil, grease & Equipment. 35 Rifles and 1500 feet to stock for Divnl. Baths. Visited 7th Corps Ammunition Salvage Dump & Divnl Grenade Dump.	
	7/2/18		Proceeded to Forward Area with D.A.D.M.S. & called at 96th Bde H.Q. & 96th Bde Kitchens & Medicines. Went to outskirts of Langemarck & back by Widgendrift, Lancia x roads, Kitchener Street & Ervichoek.	
	8/2/18		Rec'd Bulk Clothing, Boots & Stable necessaries. Also 10 Two Wheel Carrying — 200 Home Reprinters.	MM

Army Form C. 2118.

WAR DIARY
or
INTELLIGENCE SUMMARY
(Erase heading not required.)

Instructions regarding War Diaries and Intelligence Summaries are contained in F. S. Regs., Part II. and the Staff Manual respectively. Title Pages will be prepared in manuscript.

Place	Date	Hour	Summary of Events and Information	Remarks and references to Appendices
In The Field	9/2/18		No stores up from Base. Visited D.A.D.O.S. 35" Div., Ebersbergh Schongau Transp + Railhead.	
	10/2/18		Received Buck Horseshoes. Receiving Sunday. Leave allotment for my very first draft. Leave 4 men on leave at once. Proceed to 22 Army Reinforcement School. Found templates limits of the Div + handed in S.U. Rifle. Very difficult to get any more days at our work.	
	11/2/18		No stores up from Base. Arranged for return of the surplus stores in the trenches of the two battalions visited them today.	
	12/2/18		No stores from Base. Visited Field Cashier at II Corps HQ. Also D.A.D.O.S. I Div. Collected anti-aircraft sights from him.	
	13/2/18		Received Bulk Equipment Outfits, Oil grease, frosting gear. Visited D.A.D.O.S. II Corps on return from II Div. visited Lewis gun school at 2 Corps.	
	14/2/18		No stores from Base. Ordinary Routine work.	
	15/2/18		Received Bulk Clothing & State receiving. Played in a Football match for D.H.Q.	
	16/2/18		No stores from Base. Visited forward area again with Sapper — called at 96 Regt. Bde HQrs & the Bty. Had everything to the approaching Raid. They both said the recent Snow inundated with water to be further seen by return.	

Army Form C. 2118.

WAR DIARY
or
INTELLIGENCE SUMMARY
(Erase heading not required.)

Instructions regarding War Diaries and Intelligence Summaries are contained in F. S. Regs., Part II. and the Staff Manual respectively. Title Pages will be prepared in manuscript.

Place	Date	Hour	Summary of Events and Information	Remarks and references to Appendices
In the Field	17/2/18		No stores up from Base. Railhead now at Krusidorn. Nothing to Report.	
	18/2/18		Received Bulk Horseshoes & necessaries. Failed Transport of N.T. # 21 & 16. N.Z." on disbandment. Checked same & handing over to Base charge under Kherdingta Salvage Dump. Field Cashier & Corps R.O. at O.T.S. Latter was out.	
	19/2/18		Received Bolt Drilling, rod, pierce, equipment, pulley, & picketing gear. Went to 4 Army Supply School re Army Heavy mobile shops & Take Rifle, & Binoculars for repair respectively.	
	20/2/18			
	21/2/18		No stores up from Base. Nothing to Report.	
	22/2/18		Received Bulk Clothing, Boots, State necessaries Sundry. Sent 3 lorries to 4 Army Park to collect 12 - 6" Newton Mortars complete (delivered same day). T.M.B.'s driving Routine book.	
	23/2/18		Car situation absolutely impossible & can't do any job properly. Only two cars in working order on the firm.	
	24/2/18		Received Bulk Horseshoes & necessaries & letters about as there is no means of getting round.	
	25/2/18		No stores from Base. Lorries of Stores handed on to 16 N.Z. & 17 N.Z. on Thomas to despatch of instrument. That Truck will be available in tz 16 N.Z. & 17 N.Z. an instrument.	

2449 Wt. W14957/M90 750,000 1/16 J.B.C. & A. Forms/C.2118/12.

Army Form C. 2118.

WAR DIARY
or
INTELLIGENCE SUMMARY
(Erase heading not required.)

Instructions regarding War Diaries and Intelligence Summaries are contained in F. S. Regs., Part II. and the Staff Manual respectively. Title Pages will be prepared in manuscript.

Place	Date	Hour	Summary of Events and Information	Remarks and references to Appendices
In the field	26/2/18		No stores from Base. Despatches Returned stores to Base from "17" H.L.I.. Received 12 2" T.M. ets from T.M.B." in exchange for 16 "B.6" Newtons. Went to R.P. Wrought Iron Rifle for Lewis Party.	16" M 75
	27/2/18		Received Bulk Dubbin, oil & grease. Attended a conference of D.A.D.O.S at office of D.A.D.O.S. II Corps. Received instructions to prepare a scheme for the safe removal of Ordnance stores & selection of new site for Dump in case of a retirement in face of the enemy.	
	28/2/18		No stores up from Base. Despatches 12-2" T.M." received to Base on receipt of 12. 6" T.M." tested D.A.D.O.S. 3rd Dr to arrange for handing over of 2 G.S. wagon complete Harness Batts to Ours.	

M Murdoch Capt.
D.A.D.O.S. 32nd Div.

28/2/18.

Army Form C. 2118.

WAR DIARY
or
INTELLIGENCE SUMMARY
(Erase heading not required.)

WO 95 32?? / 95 324

Place	Date	Hour	Summary of Events and Information	Remarks and references to Appendices
Ikhi Aud	1.3.18		1 Tons of Pond Stores received	
"	2.3.18		Equip. Suf. Ones were drawn from 2nd Corps Salvage to meet Cof Orders	
"	3.3.18		4 Tons of Pond Stores received & 1 Army Load of Salvage returned to Railhead	
"	4.3.18		Cash Repayment forwarded to 14 Orders Depot on 14 days Arab Drivers — Arrangement with AD to send drivers of Rest Camp on the return of returnees. This Army Corps to arrange transport for same	
"	5.3.18		1 Army cart to St Jean the Besgee to totch 50 dummy figures — 511 pairs of Gum Boots were returned to Railhead & 1 Load Salvage. Arrears received for Govt Relief Disbursement	
"	6.3.18		5 Tons of Pond Stores received	
"	7.3.18		511 pairs of Boots Gum Thigh were returned to Base. As "U" HQ B^n reorganized into HQ Bn	
"	8.3.18		4 Tons of Pond Stores. Issues also 2 R.E. limbers Major Tothro	
"	9.3.18		Redesignate Army Mil Bn were submitted to all. Of Stores due to Mepon Gen I Load	
"	10.3.18		6 Tons of Salvage returning to Railhead. 3 Carts Cuts Ritarian amphor Transport of 2nd M.H. repts returns to Railhead & 1 Load Salvage. 8 pairs Gum Sockles 16 M.E. I returned to fit	
"	11.3.18		3 limbers B Wagons & Harness complete to 16 M.E. I returned to Base	
"	12.3.18		Approving Equipt complete unit 16 M.E. I handed in. No stores up from the Base	
"	13.3.18		6 Tons of General Stores and 2 Wagons MS received	
"	14.3.18		No stores received from Railhead. The 16 M.E. I handed in amphor equip in common from an Infantry to a Pioneer Bn	

2449 Wt. W14957/M90 750,000 1/16 J.B.C. & A. Forms/C.2118/12.

WAR DIARY or INTELLIGENCE SUMMARY

Army Form C. 2118.

Place	Date	Hour	Summary of Events and Information	Remarks and references to Appendices
In the Field	15/3/18		5 Tons of Hand Stores & 3 Tons of Clothing received. 1 Load of Salvage returned to Railhead.	
- do -	18/3/18		6 Tons of Hand Stores & 1 R.T. Body received.	
- do -	19/3/18		No stores received.	
- do -	19/3/18		}	
- do -	20/3/18		4 Tons of Hand Stores received. Capt. Urquhart reported as Chaplain of Ammn. Coms. at 14 Ord. Deput. Surplus stores of 18/- Kt. 1 ton returned to Railhead also 1 Load of Salvage.	
	21/3/18		No stores from Base. Despatched 2 Loads of Salvage to Base. Visited LOTS II. Corps & Field Cashier & paid out the men.	
	22/3/18		No stores from Base. Visited Salvage Dump. Ordinary Routine Work.	
	23/3/18		Received a few stores from Base. Gun Park. Ume from Base.	
	24/3/18		Received Bulk. Clothing, Boots & stable necessaries from Base. Sent of 2 Loads of Salvage to Base. Also received 1 R.T. Body for 10" A+S & Influenza & 2 Thicken R.F. to Lynet Cozies.	
	25/3/18		No stores from Base. Despatches two loads salvage to Base & cancelled same from Base in view of move.	

MW.

Army Form C. 2118.

WAR DIARY
or
INTELLIGENCE SUMMARY

(Erase heading not required.)

Instructions regarding War Diaries and Intelligence Summaries are contained in F. S. Regs., Part II. and the Staff Manual respectively. Title Pages will be prepared in manuscript.

Place	Date	Hour	Summary of Events and Information	Remarks and references to Appendices
In the Field.	26/3/18.		Received Bulk Horse shoe & necessaries from Base. A/2nd Lgt Hartley left Petn. badly wounded at Railhead one lorry driver killed & the second driver wounded. Reported casualties to all concerned.	
	27/3/18.		Dismissed most of the staff & sent lots etc to 4 Army Depot at Cayeux & had men attached to Employment Company. Sent 5 lorries to Salouel & Base & had lorries loaded up ready & had a truck at Railhead to load stores in to new area, leaving 4 lorry loads to come in by road.	
	28/3/18.		Loaded truck & conveyed it to new Railhead. Started up the lorries with remaining stores & came in by road) to Bermonville, resting for an hour at Allers. Arrived about 5 p.m. without mishap. Drivers appreciated lorries at 8.30 p.m. Armee arriving rain & kept them out all night till 6 a.m.	
	29/3/18.		Lorries rested till noon when drivers again took two & kept them out till midnight & 4 a.m. respectively. Visited Appx VI Corps in the afternoon.	

[signature]

WAR DIARY
or
INTELLIGENCE SUMMARY

(Erase heading not required.)

Place	Date	Hour	Summary of Events and Information	Remarks and references to Appendices
In the Field.	30/5/16		Sent Lorries to Railhead & see if Truck had arrived. Not there. to wired to R.T.O. Marquidon & knew if it had left there. Reply received that Truck left there 9.a.m. 25th inst. for Calais. Visited new site at 9pm at Wimerecamp.	
	31/5/16		Went on ahead with 3 marquees men to pitch camp for new Dump & sent lorries on to collect the stores. Dumped office in small room for the night & got the camp pitched well straight. Truck not arrived to wired Calais & Traffic Havrincourt & Hazebr.	

M. Urquhart Capt
D A D O S
32 Div

Army Form C. 2118.

WAR DIARY
or
INTELLIGENCE SUMMARY
(Erase heading not required.)

WO95 32 A
Vol 25

Place	Date	Hour	Summary of Events and Information	Remarks and references to Appendices
In The Field.	1/4/18		Truck not arrived yet. Tried Calais & was informed truck would be forwarded to Abbeville tomorrow. Got some Rfc Proprietors from XII Corps Troops. Sent two lorries to Dieusen to bring forward R.E. material from Back area. Found an office settled in.	
	2/4/18		Went to Lorry Berlette Railhead to see if arrangements could be made there for landing back to Base the second Blankets of the 3 Brigades which detrained there (+ stores). The second Blanket & Haversacks could not arrange as there is only an ammunition Railhead. Received 200 Bgn Refrigerators from VII. Corps Troops on loan. Truck not yet arrived. Tried Abbeville 4 tractor trucks on arrival there.	
	3/4/18		No Truck received yet. Sent Lorry Khan from Park Stores from O.O. VII Corps Troops Kasgain in the afternoon to collect 50 Tubs CL & 20 Shelter Sheets. Gurkhas captured Ayette last night about 100 prisoners & 10 machine guns.	
	4/4/18		Received Bulk clothing from Rouen. No trace of missing Truck. Can get no news of it. Q sent me to send my store leloop back to Tindicourt Kendrau at H.Q. myself. Persuaded them that we must either all stay forward at So Inch, or go back. They decided no would go back. Proceeded to Billets.	

MW

Army Form C. 2118.

WAR DIARY
or
INTELLIGENCE SUMMARY
(Erase heading not required.)

Instructions regarding War Diaries and Intelligence Summaries are contained in F.S. Regs., Part II. and the Staff Manual respectively. Title Pages will be prepared in manuscript.

Place	Date	Hour	Summary of Events and Information	Remarks and references to Appendices
In the Field	5/4/16		Received 8 vans General stores from Base. Found good store kept office at Pradicourt. As toilets for men, I have my own 6 tents- which will do. Proceeded to Corps Headquarters to see the A.D.O.S.	
	6/4/16		Moved down to Indicourt- received 6 tons General stores from Base including 27 bags vegetables. Goods car is before due at 9 a.m. each morning. Richard is himself again. Visited Dumb Loop & Railhead. Also Baths at Beuvillers. Look some rifle oil urgently required to the 3 Brigade Transport Lines. No stores up from Base.	
	7/4/16		Visited Railhead & Dump puf. also Staff Capt R.A. & O.C. D.A.C. As tent of two cwts. of returned clothing salvage stores from Base.	
	8/4/16		Visited Railhead received 8 Tons General stores including 32 wheel & Dubbin which were urgently required. Proceeded to D.H.Q. and to see A.D.O.S VI Corps.	
	9/4/16		No stores from Base. Visited Railhead and D.H.Q. also H.Q. 14r 96 Infy Bde and arranged to sent lorry to collect & captured German mortar from 14 Infy Bde H.Q.	
	10/4/16		Visited Railhead at D.H.Q. No stores up. Proceeded to Doullens for local Purchase & to arrange for collection of S.D. Clothing for Gas Cases.	

MW

Army Form C. 2118.

WAR DIARY
or
INTELLIGENCE SUMMARY

(Erase heading not required.)

Instructions regarding War Diaries and Intelligence Summaries are contained in F. S. Regs., Part II. and the Staff Manual respectively. Title Pages will be prepared in manuscript.

Place	Date	Hour	Summary of Events and Information	Remarks and references to Appendices
In The Field.	12/4/18		No stores from Base. Proceeded after strenuous efforts of the last fortnight that my lost truck has off loaded at Calais in error. D.A.D.R.T is neither truthful or competent at Calais. Visited D.H.Q. Visited D.H.Q. & no 32 M.G. Batt.	
	13/4/18.		Received old clothing from Rouen.	
	14/4/18.		Received 7 tons General Stores from Havre. Visited Railhead D.H.Q. & A.P.Q. 97 Inf Bde.	
	15/4/18.		No stores up from Base. Visited Railhead and D.H.Q. and D.D.S.T. Corps. Nothing to Report.	
	16/4/18.		No stores from Base.	
	17/4/18.		No stores from Base. Visited Railhead & D.H.Q. & proceeded to Doullens for local purchase.	
	18/4/18.		Received 7 tons old clothing & 7 tons general stores from Havre. Proceeded from Railhead to D.H.Q. on to Doullens. Purchase permit urgently required.	
	19/4/18		No stores from Base. Visited D.H.Q. who required more white paint forthwith. Went to Doullens & got some. Got the T.R.F. to pay for it.	
	20/4/18		Received 7 tons General Stores from Havre. More paint required. Got it in Doullens. Had to pay for this out of my own pocket. MH.	

2449 Wt. W14957/M90 750,000 1/16 J.B.C. & A. Forms/C.2118/12.

WAR DIARY or INTELLIGENCE SUMMARY

Army Form C. 2118.

Place	Date	Hour	Summary of Events and Information	Remarks and references to Appendices
In the Field	21/4/18		No stores up from Base. Visited Railhead + DHQ. Running of forseen coming out of kit. Attended a conference at DDOS office re return of surplus clothing.	
	22/4/18		Received 9 tons General Stores from Base. Visited DHQ + Railhead + also 17 Bde HQ + Baths at Pernois.	
	23/4/18		No stores from Base. Running of relief continued. Not yet known where we are to go to.	
	24/4/18		Received [crossed out] 9 + 5 tons General Stores from Base. We are to take over from Guards Divn at Boscourt [?] sent ODOS Guards Divn + arranged to take over his camp.	
	25/4/18		Received 6 tons Clothing from Rouen. Received two extra Lorries from M.T.Cy for the move.	
	26/4/18		No stores from Base. Railhead moved to Gary. Nothing to report.	
	27/4/18		Received 8 tons General Stores from Stores. Proceeded to Bullens for local Purchase. 7 tons Clothing from Rouen.	
	28/4/18		Received 9 tons General Stores from Havre and 4 Vehicles. Despatched a truck 1 Blankets to Base.	

Army Form C. 2118.

WAR DIARY
or
INTELLIGENCE SUMMARY
(Erase heading not required.)

Instructions regarding War Diaries and Intelligence Summaries are contained in F. S. Regs., Part II. and the Staff Manual respectively. Title Pages will be prepared in manuscript.

Place	Date	Hour	Summary of Events and Information	Remarks and references to Appendices
In the Field	29/6/18		Received 10 tons General Stores from Havre and railed Railhead + all three Brigade H.Q. Qrs.	
	30/6/18		Received 5 tons clothing + rations Railhead, 20 OTS XI Corps & 20 VI Corps troops.	

Murphant Capt.
D.A.D.T.S.
32nd Div.

WAR DIARY or INTELLIGENCE SUMMARY

Army Form C. 2118.

Vol 26

Place	Date	Hour	Summary of Events and Information	Remarks and references to Appendices
In the Field	1/5/18		Went to Railhead and obtained as much for the despatch of horse rugs. One truck of rugs etc received from Rouen. Called at 96th Brigade on the way back.	
"	2/5/18		No stores received from Base. One truck of horse rugs despatched. Visited 96th Brigade Headquarters — no Brigade Headquarters — no Brigade Headquarters.	
"	3/5/18		Surveyed Salvage Dump and 14th Brigade Headquarters. Received 15 tons of Horsy chees, memo, dubbin etc from Base. Despatched three lorry loads of returned winter clothing and Salvage. Proceeded to Etinehem to purchase certain stores urgently required.	
"	4/5/18		3 tons of clothing and detail received from Base. Three lorry loads of returned winter clothing to Railway despatched. Visited Headquarters 96th, 97th & 14th Brigades in the Afternoon. Proceeded to Doullens in the evening to purchase medal ribbons & urgently required for presentation on 6th inst.	

Army Form C. 2118.

WAR DIARY
or
INTELLIGENCE SUMMARY
(Erase heading not required.)

Instructions regarding War Diaries and Intelligence Summaries are contained in F. S. Regs., Part II. and the Staff Manual respectively. Title Pages will be prepared in manuscript.

Place	Date	Hour	Summary of Events and Information	Remarks and references to Appendices
In the field	5/5/18		No stores received from Base and no units clothing or salvage dispatched. Proceeded to Heavy mobile workshops with Pneumatic compressor for repairs and to obtain tools for thrashing machine from Tripoli.	
"	6/5/18		Six tons of Picketing Gear, Buckets, Latrine tubs washing etc. received from Base, two lorry loads of Jerbanes returned to Base. Visited 14th Brigade Headquarters.	
"	7/5/18		No stores received from Base. On lorry load of salvage despatched. 20 sets of Pack Saddling drawn from No.0 3rd Army Corps No 4.	
"	8/5/18		Seven tons of Boots, overcoats, drawers cotton, Stringing Stores to Corps. from Base, One loads of oats, agn. and Verdine returned. Six item two Pickling Gear, oil, Soap, Grease, 22 Bicycles and detail received from Base, One load of salvage and Salvage dump.	
"	10/5/18		Seven tons of Horseshoes detail received from Base also two tons water. Visited railhead (Group) Salvage dump 91/5 Borders.	

2449 Wt. W14957/M90 750,000 1/16 J.B.C. & A. Forms/C.2118/12.

WAR DIARY
or
INTELLIGENCE SUMMARY

Army Form C. 2118.

(Erase heading not required.)

Place	Date	Hour	Summary of Events and Information	Remarks and references to Appendices
In the Field	10/5/18		Two lorry loads of Returned Work Shop Stores Lines dispatched to Base.	
"	11/5/18		Seven tons of clothing retailed from Base, three lorry loads of worn and underclothing returned. Visited washing and salvage dump.	
"	12/5/18		Cox Respirators, Picketing Gear etc received. Two lorry loads of winter clothing stores of salvage dispatched. A.A.G. moved to Pettoncourt. D.A.D.O.S. during night of 13/14 inspected at Bainnont. Audits the Salvage form loads dispatched.	
"	13/5/18		Visited A.D.S. 6th Corps and heavy mobile Workshops - Auxi-les-	
"	14/5/18		Chateaux in the morning and Advanced Headquarters and Salvage Dump during the afternoon. Eight tons of stores received from Base, one Covered Gun Emplacement and stable necessaries. One lorry load of salvage dispatched.	
"	15/5/18		Five tons of Boots and necessaries received from here and one lorry load of salvage one of Jerkins dispatched.	
"	16/5/18		Six tons of stores received from Base - Oil, Grease, Dubbins, Webb and 70 Food Containers. One load of winter clothing dispatched.	

MC

Army Form C. 2118.

WAR DIARY
or
INTELLIGENCE SUMMARY
(Erase heading not required.)

Instructions regarding War Diaries and Intelligence Summaries are contained in F. S. Regs., Part II. and the Staff Manual respectively. Title Pages will be prepared in manuscript.

Place	Date	Hour	Summary of Events and Information	Remarks and references to Appendices
In The Field	17/5/16.		Visited Divnl H.Qrs. & H.Qrs. 96th Inf.Bde. Received Bulk Horse Shoes & small quantity of Horse Shoes. Lieut. Clarke returned & proceeded to 37th Divn. Took him over in the Car & handed him over safely.	
	18/5/16.		Received Bulk Clothing. Visited Railhead. Ordnance H.Q.r. & Salvage Dump. Also 96th Bde H.Q.	
	19/5/16		Received 5 tons General Stores. Proceeded to Army Mobile Shop & Ordnance Workshops & Telescope regarding which has been collected. Prismatic Compass & Telescope regarding which has been repaired & visited Divn. H.Q. in the afternoon.	
	20/5/16.		No stores from Base. Sent away 2 loads of returned Clothing & Boots to Base. Visited D.H.Q. & Depot Battalion & Salvage Dump	
	21/5/16.		Received 6 tons General Stores & sent away 2 loads of returned stores. D.H.Q. & 14th Inf Bde H.Q. Also Depot Battalion & Salvage Dump.	
	22/5/16		Received 3 tons clothing. Visited Railhead & A.D.O.S. & Corps H.Q. Sent away 1 load returns.	
	23/5/16		Received 5 tons General Stores. Proceeded to Railhead. H.Qrs. D.A.C. & Salvage Dump. Also 92nd Fd.Amb. Sent away 1 load Returns. Received notification that Lieut. Dawson was struck down for instruction.	

MW.

Army Form C. 2118.

WAR DIARY
or
INTELLIGENCE SUMMARY

(Erase heading not required.)

Instructions regarding War Diaries and Intelligence Summaries are contained in F.S. Regs., Part II. and the Staff Manual respectively. Title Pages will be prepared in manuscript.

Place	Date	Hour	Summary of Events and Information	Remarks and references to Appendices
In the Field	24/5/18		Received 2 Tons General Stores from Havre. Also 36 Lewis Guns for 9 Battalions making a total of 28 guns per Batt. Proceeded to Doullens to fetch Lieut. Lannon who is attached to this Div. for instruction in the duties of D.A.D.O.S. Received 3 Lewis Guns from Gun Park to replace U/S. Visited Salvage Dump.	
	25/5/18		Received 6 Tons General Stores from Havre and 7 Tons clothing from Rouen. including 300 suits for fatigue changes. Visited D.H.Q. Railhead & O.C. D.A.C.	
	26/5/18		No stores from Base. Visited Corps H.Q. & stayed for 2 hrs. with A.D.O.S. Officers gathering knowledge of A.D.O.S. work. Visited D.H.Q. & Salvage Dump.	
	27/5/18		Received 8 Tons General Stores. Visited Salvage Dump & Depot Battalion & D.H.Q. Proceeded to Corps H.Q. for instruction.	
	28/5/18		No stores from Base. Visited D.H.Q. & H.Q. Divl Artillery.	
	29/5/18		Received 4 Tons Clothing from Rouen & 1 G. Wagon & one Interpart. Proceeded to D.H.Q. to make Salvage Dump & Q.M. store in Company with D.A.P.M.G. Proceeded to Authieu & Frevent for local Purchase.	
	30/5/18		Received 6 Tons General Stores. Visited D.H.Q. and 40 & 41 & all three Brigades & the Div. with D.APMG & Div Sanitar. also Depot Bat. & Salvage Dump. for visits into III Corps.	M.C.

Army Form C. 2118.

WAR DIARY
or
INTELLIGENCE SUMMARY

(Erase heading not required.)

Place	Date	Hour	Summary of Events and Information	Remarks and references to Appendices
In the field	2/5/19		Visited A.H.Q. & Salvage Dump. Received 8 tons General Stores. Also stores V. Despatched truck containing winter clothing (blankets) MM. 2/5/19	

Army Form C. 2118.

WAR DIARY
or
INTELLIGENCE SUMMARY
(Erase heading not required.)

Instructions regarding War Diaries and Intelligence Summaries are contained in F.S. Regs., Part II. and the Staff Manual respectively. Title Pages will be prepared in manuscript.

Vol 27

Place	Date	Hour	Summary of Events and Information	Remarks and references to Appendices
4th Div Train Field	1/6/18		Visited Corps Troops. R.H.Q. and Salvage Dump. Despatched truck of Blankets to Base. Capt Urquhart left for VII Corps to take up duties of A.D.O.S.	
	2/6/18		Visited R.H.Q. and Corps Troops. Four lorry loads of "Salvage" (including quantity of blankets) sent to Base. Six Wagons received from Base.	
	3/6/18		Nothing received from Base. Despatched two lorry loads of Unserviceable Clothing to Base. Visited Moullins and called at A.T.Q.	
	4/6/18		Received 10 Zone General Stores P. I.V. lorry Clothing. Two lorry loads of "Salvage" (including Blankets) despatched before Nine No. 0794 received from R.H.Q. No car available in afternoon.	
	5/6/18		Despatched 1½ lorry loads of U/S Clothing. Nothing received from Base. Visited R.H.Q. Salvage Dump & H.Q. 96 Brigade, and returned via Frevent.	
	6/6/18		Visited D.H.Q. Divisional General, A.R.Q.M.G. inspected Stores P. Mens & Womens. Frevent & Moullins. Despatched one lorry containing U/S Clothing. Received 6 Zone O.R.I. Grass. No car available.	
	7/6/18		Nothing sent to or from Base.	

2449 Wt. W14957/M90 750,000 1/16 J.B.C. & A. Forms/C.2118/12.

Army Form C. 2118.

WAR DIARY
or
INTELLIGENCE SUMMARY

(Erase heading not required.)

Instructions regarding War Diaries and Intelligence Summaries are contained in F. S. Regs., Part II. and the Staff Manual respectively. Title Pages will be prepared in manuscript.

Place	Date	Hour	Summary of Events and Information	Remarks and references to Appendices
In the Field	8/6/18		Visited Baths Officer & D.A.D.O. Called at H.Q. of 96th, 114th and 95th Brigade with A.D.M.S. Received 4 lorry loads Clothing Laundry & Necessaries & One Cart Load Light (ref D.H.Q. Q 15/14)	
	9/6/18		Despatched 3 lorry loads of u/s Clothing (including Blankets) to Base and received 6 lorry loads Shirts & Refitting Gear. Called at Corps Troops. Sent two lorry loads of unserviceable clothing to Base. No car available.	
	10/6/18		Visited D.H.Q. & Headquarters Machine Gun Battalion. Also called at C.R.E.'s office and on return journey called on Police Officer Salvage Dump & 92 Field Ambulance (equipment &c). Nackatches One lorry load of Received 6 lorry from Havre (equipment &c). Nackatches One lorry load of unserviceable clothing to Base.	
	11/6/18		Called at D.H.Q. & on C.R.E. Visited Havre to make purchase & proceeded to Heavy Motor Workshops with Police Officer & was prevented from Base & despatched One lorry load of u/s Clothing. 37 Lewis Guns & 1 Vickers received for Gun Park.	

WAR DIARY
or
INTELLIGENCE SUMMARY

(Erase heading not required.)

Army Form C. 2118

Place	Date	Hour	Summary of Events and Information	Remarks and references to Appendices
In the Field	13/6/18		Called at R.H.Q. & Salvage Co. Visited D.A.B. Headquarters. Despatched One lorry load of U/S Clothing to Base.	
	14/6/18		Called on Gas Officer & then at Salvage Dump. Visited Border Regt. & 15th K.L.S. stores & then returned. Received 6 tons Petrol, Oil & Grease & despatched 1 lorry load of U/S Clothing.	
	15/6/18		Sent One lorry load of U/S Clothing to Base. Called at R.H.Q. & then visited No. 2 Co. Iron & OC Corps Troops (Collected 3 Elliptical Springs) & R.A.O.C. Corps. Received a visit at Store from R.A.O.C. Corps.	
	16/6/18		Received 5 tons Clothing from Base & sent down One lorry load U/S Clothing. Visited R.H.Q. & A/Yst Battalion & then called at Third Army Troops Nos 1 & 2 afterwards called on R.A.O.C. Corps. Received 26 Lewis Guns from Gun Park.	
	19/6/18		Received 5 tons Horse Shoes, Mobile Measures from, & despatched One lorry load U/S Clothing to Base. Being unsuccessful in obtaining articles required by A.A.Q.M.G. (for Gen. l. H. Btn.) proceeded to Abbeville but unable to succeed. On the way called at Heavy Mobile Workshops to collect Perroculars & two Compass for repair. Purchased 24 Flat Irons.	

Army Form C. 2118

WAR DIARY
or
INTELLIGENCE SUMMARY
(Erase heading not required.)

Instructions regarding War Diaries and Intelligence Summaries are contained in F. S. Regs., Part II. and the Staff Manual respectively. Title Pages will be prepared in manuscript.

Place	Date	Hour	Summary of Events and Information	Remarks and references to Appendices
In the Field	18/6/18		Called on Postal Officer at A.H.Q. & H.Q. Machine Gun Battalion. Collected stores at Corps Salvage Dump & them 2 Monkey Puzzle Mountings & from Corps troops. Despatched 1 lorry load of W/S Clothing to Base: nothing received.	
	19/6/18		Called at D.H.Q.: on the way had accident - car slightly damaged. Received loads of Camp Equipt & Accoutrements. On truck of Salvage sent to Base. Called on Salvage Officer, then proceeded to D.H.Q. ag[t] which visited H.Q. of three Infantry Brigades. Called at M.T. Co. & Field Cashier (to money to pay). Made some local purchases at Arvaou.	
	20/6/18		Received 8 Iron Oil & Grease & Anchokes. Despatched 2 Lorry loads of W/S Clothing to Base. No Car available. Visited N.L.6 & No 2 Co. Team.	
	21/6/18		Visited D.H.Q. and on return called on Postal & Salvage Officer. Collected 2 Monkey Puzzle Mountings of Corps troops & attempted to obtain stores from R.O.O. Frohly, but with no success. Despatched 1 load of W/S Clothing to Base.	2
	22/6/18		No car available. Received 6 Iron General Stores? and 1 lorry load of Clothing to Base. Pte Barnshall left for Corps troops.	9
	24/6/18		Called at D.H.Q. & Salvage. Proceeded to Corps troops & returned. Received 6 some Boots. Marsoaus to D.A.D.S.S. called.	

WAR DIARY
or
INTELLIGENCE SUMMARY

Army Form C. 2118

Place	Date	Hour	Summary of Events and Information	Remarks and references to Appendices
In the Field	25/6/18		No car available.	
	26/6/18		Called at D.H.Q. & Salvage. Despatched 2 lorry loads of U/s Clothing to base. Proceeded to Third Army Troops Not (for canvas) & then to Avelino to pick up Lieut Purchas. Received 2 G.S. Wagons & two lorry loads of U/s Clothing.	
	27/6/18		Received 5 horse General Store from Havre: despatched one load of harness to Base. Visited D.H.Q. with Lieut Purchas. accompanied by Lieut Purchas visited a Brigade Hqrs. (96, 14 & 99) and on return journey called at D.H.Q. & Salvage. No stores received: despatched one lorry load of U/s Clothing	
	28/6/18		Called at H.Q. D.A.L. & Not C. also No 21 3.C. train. In the afternoon visited M.L.C. (No car available until 5.30pm) Received 6 Lame Horses to 1 despatched one lorry load of U/s Clothing	
	30/6/18		No time R. Lieut H.N. Rawson left for 5th Army H.L.S.L. Lieut L. H. Purchas became acting DAP83. Bought 8 Hackmore at Anne	

Ruthercroft
acting DAP83
37 Div.

War Diary
of
D.A.D.O.S.
32nd Division

Vol 3 – No. 7 (July 1918)

Army Form C. 2118

WAR DIARY
or
INTELLIGENCE SUMMARY
(Erase heading not required.)

WS 28

Place	Date	Hour	Summary of Events and Information	Remarks and references to Appendices
In the Field	1/7/18		Two trucks received containing 6 tons clothing - 6 tons general stores. No car available to visit Gs salvage.	
	2/7/18		Visited DAQMG re to get RE shells approved. Attempted to purchase luminous paint. None available in local towns. Obtained some from Special Coy R.E. Visited Salvage dump. No truck.	
	3/7/18			
	4/7/18		Truck general stores 5 tons received. Borrowed 2 Bowser Stores from VI Corps Hos. To be returned on 7th inst. Visited HQ 7s Division - Salvage & Canteen. Issued 9 Bowser Stores - 30 food containers & about 250 tin cups on loan to Canteen. No truck.	
	5/7/18 6/7/18		Truck of clothing & necessaries - about 5 tons received. No car available.	
	7/7/18		Sent 1 OO & 3 OS Army troops No 4 to collect 100 sets of clothing under authority 3rd Army O/28/84 of 2/7/18. VI Corps Q/855 of 3/7/18. Owner considered load too much for 2 slings - so put the clothing on one of my lorries that was collecting 30 meat safes for 7s Sn Sec. One truck & 2 horses lorries 6 tons.	

Army Form C. 2118.

WAR DIARY
or
INTELLIGENCE SUMMARY
(Erase heading not required.)

Instructions regarding War Diaries and Intelligence Summaries are contained in F.S. Regs., Part II. and the Staff Manual respectively. Title Pages will be prepared in manuscript.

Place	Date	Hour	Summary of Events and Information	Remarks and references to Appendices
	8.7.18		Returned humours found to Stream Cy R.E. Returned 2 days stores to O.O. I Corps tps. M.O. truck. A.I.A. arranged for inspection of Armourers & Ammunition Shops.	
	9.7.18		M.O. truck. Visited Salvage & collected 2 discharger Cups, Walkers better-hearing magazine	
	10.7.18		M.O. truck. Visited Douceres & bought 10 metres wire gauze. A.I.A. continued on D.A.D.O.S. & promoted Lewis major to his 2nd employed.	
	11.7.18		M.O. truck. Visited Rurale. A+5 Hours 20 July 29.	
	12.7.18		2 trucks – 6 tons Clothing. 6 tons General Stores. Visited 4 R.O.Co & 9 CCS 97 T.M.B. and collected 5 tons Armourers prifmate – 2 companies pneumatic of Rerolin.	
	13.7.18		M.O. truck. Visited 3 T.M.Bs. Royal Scots, 4/5 & 4 R.G. Royal Irish, 16 R.aus, 15 R.aus) and 2nd Manchesters and 91st Field Ambulance.	
	14.7.18		be truck. Clothing received. Visited Salvage & collected 4 Lewis gun magazines. Visited C.R.E. & O.C. Signals. Visited by A.D.O.O. VI Corps and Struck stabs. Received electrify gear (3 tons) 200 R.2. binoculars pismatic & one Company prismatic to 3rd Army heavy shop for repair.	
	15.7.18		Bought sandgloves wick for C.P. lamps for G. office. Also 24 Items	
	16.7.18		M.O. truck. Visited C.R.A. 518 Field Coy R.E. W.O. & 161 Acc R.F.A. A/161. 16 M. L.G. & 70 Field Ambulance.	

2449 Wt. W14957/M90 750,000 1/16 J.B.C. & A. Forms/C.2118/12.

WAR DIARY or INTELLIGENCE SUMMARY

Army Form C. 2118.

Place	Date	Hour	Summary of Events and Information	Remarks and references to Appendices
In the Field.	17.7.18		Visited Salvage 2, 3 & 4 Corps trains. 219 Field Coy RE. 92 Field Ambulances. Depot Bn. Dumps of equipment (4 tons) received. Handed over to Above II Corps one Lewis gun tripod.	
	18.7.18		Returned all items in Salvage dump to Railhead. Area Stores, ie. Iron fochr. surplus Emergency Amm Carriers. Reserve Gas Clothing. Rack huts. Carrying water tins to 00 II Corps tps. Renor - divisions moving.	
	19.7.18		Moved from II Corps to X Corps area. Additional 3 lorries were required to move everything. i.e. reserve of S.R.R. Armourers Shop etc. Lorries were supplied by 'Q'. Railhead ROUSBRUGGE. Moved new Base receipt from 21st Div.	
	20.7.18		Visited Heavy Mobile Shops - 96 Bde HdQrs.	
	21.7.18		Discovered the 3rd lorry promised by "Q" for removal of amn has not supplied, sent lorry back to collect balance of stores.	
	22.7.18		Took a list of stores left by Division at STOMER.	
	23.7.18		Visited Corps Salvage dump. Collected arms, equipment, especially	
	24.7.18		Arms. Nothing to report.	
	25.7.18			
	26.7.18		Went to get Glass for General's Car. Got the glass. 3 trucks received. 1.0 5 prs Genuine Stores	
	27.7.18		6 " Boots & Clothing 1 batch Card 467 wheels.	

Army Form C. 2118.

WAR DIARY
or
INTELLIGENCE SUMMARY

(Erase heading not required.)

Instructions regarding War Diaries and Intelligence Summaries are contained in F.S. Regs., Part II. and the Staff Manual respectively. Title Pages will be prepared in manuscript.

Place	Date	Hour	Summary of Events and Information	Remarks and references to Appendices
In the Field	29/7/18		Two Coys. to-day. 8 two horse teams & two wagons. Visited heavy mobile shop, took R. wanted for repair. Sent lorry to Calais for kits & respirators.	
	30/7/18		Visited A.O.D. 12 special respirators received from Army & issued to H.Q. Bn.	
	31/7/18		Visited gun park.	

[signature] Lieut. Col.
A.A. & D.30 Bn.

War Diary of
D.A.D.O.S.
32nd (Brit.) Division

Vol. 3 — No. 8
August 1918.

Army Form C. 2118.

DADOS 32) VIII 29

WAR DIARY
or
INTELLIGENCE SUMMARY
(Erase heading not required.)

Instructions regarding War Diaries and Intelligence Summaries are contained in F. S. Regs., Part II. and the Staff Manual respectively. Title Pages will be prepared in manuscript.

Place	Date	Hour	Summary of Events and Information	Remarks and references to Appendices
In the field	1.8.18 & 19.18		Visited 96th & 97th Coys, and Salvage Dump and A.D.O.S.	
	2.8.18		Collected 21 mountings from Heavy Art Wshops that had been repaired for R complete equipments for retain. Visited Enyor Davison while I was out. Indents states & forms for men for meals by two orders.	
			Collected 19 Sets packsaddley & 12 Yukon packs from No 3 & Army Wps No 3 Stores from Divisional Dump St Omer.	
	3.8.18		2 Trucks arrived from Base containing General Stores & Clothing for Turcos " " " new underclothing from Rio Baths " " " VI Corps " 10,000 Shirts	
			19 Sets packsaddery put on rail for VI Corps. Attended conference at ADOS VI Corps. Collected 50 trench covers from O.O. 2nd Army Wps No 3. for Bothmer.	
	4.8.18		Nothing to report.	
	5.8.18		Three trucks received.	
	6.8.18		Returned Yukon packs - 19 sets packsaddley & 50 trench covers to O.O.II Corps troops. Sent Ammonias to a 500 Respirators by truck to new destination.	
	7.8.18		Division moved to IV Army Area. (may + horses escaped)	

2449 Wt. W14957/M90 750,000 1/16 J.B.C. & A. Forms/C.2118/12.

WAR DIARY
INTELLIGENCE SUMMARY

Army Form C. 2118.

Place	Date	Hour	Summary of Events and Information	Remarks and references to Appendices
B.H.Q. Beld	8.8.18		Railhead Hangard and Domart. Lined Boxes accepted others from 95 no 1. Division moved forward. Remained at Rion H.d.Q.ts.	
"	9.8.18		Railhead SAKEUX. No lure R. 2 lorries borrowed by "Q" and returned.	
"	10.8.18		Moved Amm'n office from Cauillon to Cagny. Railhead AMIENS, no lure R. Two lorries had 1½ days journey each. Two lorries returned by "Q". No car available.	
"	11.8.18		One lorry used to collect rations for rear H.d.Q.ts. Reconnoissanced truck from Kerrebrugge arrived at Railhead. Visited A.D.O.S. Can. Corps. One lorry to O.O. IV Army. No. 1 to collect 1 marquee, 12 C.S.t. tents for Div H.d.Q.ts. Received orders to send 2 lorries to move Div H.d.Q.ts at 4.30 a.m. 12th.	
"	12.8.18	2.30 am 6.0	Two lorries sent to Div H.d.Q.ts. Lorry sent to Div H.d.Q.ts. to deliver tents. Visited advanced D.H.Q. & Rld. to collect 20 sets pack-saddling from O.O.⁴th Army No.1. Railhead Boves. Arranged to get Lanyard to re-equip Division – Special demand carried to Base for clothing for ⅓ strength of Division.	
"	13.8.18		Two lorries sent to move Div H.d.Q.ts. One for rations. Drew 70 prs. ankle boots from O.O. IV Corps No. 1. Sent lorry to gun park to draw 3 pack ammo. Visited 97th Base H.d.Q.ts. No trouble.	
	14.8.18		Railhead AMIENS. Asked for car & am. No car supplied. No lure R. Killed Ramsons & Railhead lorry for Railhead & Harcourt. Ireland, & following C.C.S. A79 &8. 20, 4, 41	

2449 Wt. W14957/M90 750,000 1/16 J.B.C. & A. Forms/C.2118/12.

Army Form C. 2118.

WAR DIARY
or
INTELLIGENCE SUMMARY
(Erase heading not required.)

Instructions regarding War Diaries and Intelligence Summaries are contained in F. S. Regs., Part II. and the Staff Manual respectively. Title Pages will be prepared in manuscript.

Place	Date	Hour	Summary of Events and Information	Remarks and references to Appendices
In the field	14.8.18		12, 5, during afternoon. Collected 30 revolvers & 1 case for Division	
	15.8.18		private (RJ) Visited Railhead. No truck. Visited ADOS CE. Informed declaration from Gun Park, under authority from Army. Visited the 3 RE & Rev. units. Have not yet advised for freeing items. eg. Branding Iron etc. Visited 53, 55 & 61 CCS Collected 2 revolvers. Lewis Guns Loc. Visited —	
	16.8.18		7 tons of stores received at Railhead — Horseshoes & soap. Visited No 14, 41 & 12 CCS. Railheads at Vigna court, Longpré, + 00 AT No 1. Collected 43 Revolvers — 2 Bristol Key and 3 pro Bohncars.	
	17.8.18		18 tons (2 trucks) clothing received. Flares & Revolvers from 00 IV Army. Moved everybody except office staff to new Div HQ Dept.	
	18.8.18			
	19.8.18		Railhead Kleen Britonneux. At 9.30 am informed Railhead was to be Amiens again. One truck of stores received. Moved office & staff to new Div Hqrs. 18 tons of clothing left at Hotel Dio at Halfa	
	20.8.18		to be collected as soon as possible. Nothing to report.	

2449 Wt. W14957/M90 750,000 1/16 J.B.C. & A. Forms/C.2118/12.

WAR DIARY
INTELLIGENCE SUMMARY

(Erase heading not required.)

Army Form C. 2118.

Place	Date	Hour	Summary of Events and Information	Remarks and references to Appendices
In the Field	21/8/18		Rested & refreshed. Moved Clothing to new H/Qts.	
	22/8/18		Visited A. & S. Corps. D.A.D.O.S. Army & got permission to make Vickery smoke Bombs. Borrowed Dummies bombs. Brush wiping ramrod calico & thread. They were not then required.	
	23/8/18		Visited 5, 53, 55, 37 C.C.S. & collected 8 revolvers & 1 Very pistol.	
	24/8/18		7 lorry stores received. Army delivering at R.P.	
	25/8/18		Moved to Advanced H/Qts. Issued 500 suits, 6+1 D. & S. for yellowsgas men. Railhead GUILLAUCOURT from to be embarked at anything.	
	26/6/18		No train arrived. Found yesterdays train at Villers Bretonneaux. Two flats containing G.S. barrels & small arms carts for M.G. Bn. 2 baled carts sent by lorry from D.Dock. H.Q. Army as ??? Bn had informed the army they required 2 carts to replace ??? "G.V." a ?Kat. 9 Each they said were most important. All of which is untrue. The unified carts were a first issue as an additional 2. I never said they were not available. Suggest I am consulted when carts made old statements. Two lorry loads of returned stores sent to Coho. Salvage for Railhead unable to accept. All Empties being used for prisoners. Nothing to report.	
	27/8/18		True ? grass & scale as advance.	
	28/8/18			

WAR DIARY
or
INTELLIGENCE SUMMARY

Army Form C. 2118.

Place	Date	Hour	Summary of Events and Information	Remarks and references to Appendices
In the Field	29.8.18		Visited advanced Rio Volga, a Salvage.	
	30.8.18		Truck. Delivered stores at refilling point. Artillery did not turn up. Railhead to Hague. Visited adv Div HQrs. Two loads to corps Salvage.	
	31.8.18		Instruction received lunch for 2 water carts. No reply received.	

Jno Buchanan Sayer
Lab O 37 Div.

War Diary
of
D.A.D.O.S. 32nd (Brit.) Division

Vol. 3.   No 9
(September 1918)

D.A.D.O.S.
1/10/18
32nd DIVISION

Army Form C. 2118.

WAR DIARY
or
INTELLIGENCE SUMMARY
(Erase heading not required.)

Instructions regarding War Diaries and Intelligence Summaries are contained in F. S. Regs., Part II. and the Staff Manual respectively. Title Pages will be prepared in manuscript.

JB 30

Place	Date	Hour	Summary of Events and Information	Remarks and references to Appendices
	1.9.18		5 tons of clothing received. Visited the three Brigades & Div HQrs. Three lorries detd. to Div HQGs to move them. One lorry sent to Cavalry officer.	
	2.9.18		No truck. Visited A.R.P. & A.D.O. Corps. Told 3 motor cars coming the Brown farm from PaR - went to try. Cars not available. Found out what Bns had to be drawn from o/o IV Army the No I. Sent lorry to 107th Divn.	
	3.9.18		Truck of carts arrived. Visited adv Div HQrs. Lorry with water carts arrived from H.A.T. No I at 7.30 p.m. Went over to deliver to units. Arrived Bde HQrs about midnight.	
	4.9.18		Div HQrs moved to 65D.Y.33.c.7.1.6.	
	5.9.18		Railhead FRISSY. 7 tons of stores, picketing gear & horseshoe. Sent grease.	
	6.9.18		No truck. Sent 2 lorries to Div HQrs. Two lorries sent on to Bdes.	
	7.9.18		Truck scant. Two lorries taken by Div HQrs. One lorry delivered stores to DAC 9 Bde, Other to 14th & 97th. Stopped supply lorries as units unable to accept. Railhead HARCHEL Pot from 8th inst.	
	8.9.18		Nowhere ergent demand from Batteries for Horseshoes. No lorries available as all ordered by division to move near Div HQrs. Truck constantly 8 tons stores arrived.	
	9.9.18		Moved to MISERY. Evans lorries loads, as units have been unable to accept stores.	

Army Form C. 2118.

WAR DIARY
or
INTELLIGENCE SUMMARY

(Erase heading not required.)

Place	Date	Hour	Summary of Events and Information	Remarks and references to Appendices
	10.9.18		Nothing to report.	
	11.9.18		Came under G.S. Corps. No truck - Route to Gunpark Valley next Bde.	
	12.9.18		No truck	
	13.9.18		Moved to Corbie Area - 8 lorry loads stores - & took over Dump of 6th Bn Ordce	
	14.9.18		Field balance of Ordce Stores from Twisay - moved into new Dump Major Pinchard proceeded on leave.	
	15.9.18		12 Tons stores received from Railhead - sent lorry to Gun Park - Recovered vehicles 2 Wagons J.S. to BAMS 1st Bn - Tm for 32nd SAC & 1 Coy 32nd Bns Train	
16.9.18			2 lorry loads of Ordce Stores sent to SAC - 2 lorry loads of Salvage returned to Base. 36 Items Jura merchanted in Armourer's Shop	
17.9.18			5 Tons of Clothing received. 36 Lewis Guns merchanted in Armourer's Shop	
18.9.18			2 lorries with Ordce Stores sent to R.A. & 14th Kyble H.Q. 5 lorry loads of Salvage sent to Railhead. 1 lorry sent to "Q" for duty. 36 Lewis Guns were overhauled. Helpers in Armourer's Shop. Stores collected from Gun Park. Major Pinchard returned off leave.	
19.9.18			Visited 14th Bde. No truck.	
20.9.18			No truck. Visited Armourers	
21.9.18			Eight tons of Clothing received. Visited 97th Bde HQrs Royal H Bordrs & 10/HLI.	

WAR DIARY or INTELLIGENCE SUMMARY

Army Form C. 2118.

(Erase heading not required.)

Place	Date	Hour	Summary of Events and Information	Remarks and references to Appendices
	24.9.18		10 tons of stores received (including guns)	
	25.9.18		One lorry to 14's Bde, one lorry to Arty. Division arrived forward.	
	26.9.18		9 tons arrived at railhead. Reconnoitred as mining strong, or tomorrow. Received some G.S.W. & other acc about entire - car & horse a move. Issued up one lorry & found a place had been returned. Left 140.99 men.	
	26.9.18		3 ment to Getupilu. 8 range. Eight lorry loads. Visited Prestitopts stores. Limbers lorry to Batty. Railhead. CARTIER? One lorry lent to Div Batty. No truck. One lorry to Gun Park. One lorry lent to Div Batty.	
	27.9.18		Reconnoitred truck of 9 tons of stable necessaries & mines. Visited Coys. Lorry to Gun Park.	
	28.9.18		Five tons of Clothing received. Rav & lorries to D.A.P.M. No car available.	
	29.9.18		No truck. No car available.	
	30.9.18		8 tons of stores. Box respirators issued & Head Shop. Collected 130 exchangeable Hickman kits, 3 Conductors & some tubes, 17 Rifles SMLE from 24 BOS. Australian Corps tho. 6 rifles SMLE for tp to BAT no 1.	

2449 Wt. W14957/M90 750,000 1/16 J.B.C. & A. Forms/C.2118/12.

War Diary
of
D.A.D.O.S. 32nd (Brit.) Div.
Vol 3 — No 10 (Oct.r 1918)

WAR DIARY
or
INTELLIGENCE SUMMARY

Army Form C. 2118.

Place	Date	Hour	Summary of Events and Information	Remarks and references to Appendices
In the field	1.10.18		Railhead MONTIGNY FARM. Truck of coats received. Visited 47 I.C.S and collected 11 overcoats.	
	2.10.18		Visited Div HdQrs. Visited Some COs 9-0-0-11 AT No I Collected 19 Rwatus & 2 Pistols Car.	
	3.10.18		Took four mornings for Vickers machine guns to No 5 6rd Heavy Mobile shops. No truck. Lorry to 97 Bde. Lorry to AON Gunpark 9-00 IV AT No I to collect 30 sets packsaddlery for SAA Sec DAC	
	4.10.18		No truck. Lorry to Gun park. 30 sets packsaddlery delivered to SAA Sec DAC. Collected 120 trench covers from 5th Div & delivered to 96 Bde. Asked for a car. Didn't get it.	
	5.10.18		Asked for car to collect anti tank gun from Goo. Didn't get it. 5 tons of clothing received. Lorry to Gun Park. One lorry to IX CT for Vickers guns.	
	6.10.18		Railhead TINCOURT BOUCY. 3 Trucks received. 2 containing 12000 Je.Rms — 8 tons 10 tons Horseshoes. Asked for car but didn't get it.	
	7.10.18		No truck. 2 lorries sent for Bedlows - 2 collected tents & trench covers for 96th Bde. Asked for car but did not get one. Visited 14 Pole HdQrs & 16 AD.	

Army Form C. 2118.

WAR DIARY
or
INTELLIGENCE SUMMARY
(Erase heading not required.)

Instructions regarding War Diaries and Intelligence Summaries are contained in F. S. Regs., Part II. and the Staff Manual respectively. Title Pages will be prepared in manuscript.

Place	Date	Hour	Summary of Events and Information	Remarks and references to Appendices
(8.10.18 to 16 Oct)			Visited 96th Bde H.Qrs. 15 & 16 Lancs, 2/5 Manchesters, 1/6 Royal Scots, 90 Field Ambulance & M.G. Bn., 206 Field Coy. 97th Bde H.Qrs. + Div HdQrs. 2/6 A.R.S.	
	9.10.18		G. Stores General Stores received.	
	10.10.18		6 lorry loads of Salvage returned to Railhead. A.D.V.S. 9th Corps visited dump. Visited Dieppe & bought 6 lamp glasses & 101 Kilos of tinsmiths aluminium paint as we are not getting much from Base. Visited Rouen and ordered 24 Divisional signs for putting on Bde Armbands.	
	11.10.18		No truck. Lorry to Gun Park. Several loads returned entrance to Railhead.	
	12.10.18		Truck of wagons. Sent lorry to Hott Hur Kits. Visited 1 to 14th Bde to 14th Bde to Artillery.	
	13.10.18		L.P. paint arrived. Truck of 6 tons of horse shoes & overage. Lorry sent to Div HdQrs.	
	14.10.18		Truck Stores C/o. Went to Dieppe Havre & Rouen. Made arrangements to buy door paint if necessary. Brought back armbands with Div sign - Cost frs 1.00 each.	
	15.10.18		Sent lorry to Artillery. Lorry to Div HdQrs. Inspected by G.O.C. Division.	
	16.10.18		Stores Soap oil Grease & pickelling gear. Visited O.O. VI AT NoI. Railhead at Chatfield & Serqueuil & collected 4 revolvers (one since proved "VI")	

2449 Wt. W14957/M90 750,000 1/16 J.B.C. & A. Forms/C.2118/12.

WAR DIARY
or
INTELLIGENCE SUMMARY

(Erase heading not required.)

Army Form C. 2118.

Place	Date	Hour	Summary of Events and Information	Remarks and references to Appendices
In the Field	17.10.18		Railhead Montigny Farm. Truck of vehicles however arrived at Miraumont. Visited 3 CCS & 3 Railheads but got no abrasive stores.	
	18.10.18		No truck thing to 10 tons of Clothing carried. Collected 6 Binoculars from Rec. Dep. No. 2. Loads of returned ordnance to Railhead. One lorry to Guipard. One truck containing 10 tons Winter Clothing (Drawers Vests) sent out to Bas. Artillery during afternoon.	
	19.10.18			
	20.10.18		4 trucks arrived. (3 of Blankets 1 of Winter Clothing.) Railhead at ESSIGNY le PETIT. Trucks did not arrive till 6 p.m.	
	21.10.18		Moved to FRESNOY le GRAND. One truck of haversacks and 2 trucks of vehicles.	
	22.10.18		110 truck. Collected oil lub. for M.G.Bn. 5 glls from OO IX CT no 1 and 24 galls from OO IX CT no 2.	
	23.10.18		Went to Amiens to buy lamp globes. Two trucks arrived one of blankets one of winter clothing & boots.	
	24.10.18		Visited 96 Bde H.Q.6, 2 Inchesters, 154th Lanc.s. Visited 3 CCS & collected 1 Revolver 91 non-boots. Trucks (3) did not arrive till 6.15. 10 tons of Blankets received. Truck of J.S. Boots & one of Equipment	

2449 Wt. W14957/M90 750,000 1/16 J.B.C. & A. Forms/C.2118/12.

Instructions regarding War Diaries and Intelligence Summaries are contained in F. S. Regs., Part II. and the Staff Manual respectively. Title Pages will be prepared in manuscript.

WAR DIARY or INTELLIGENCE SUMMARY

Army Form C. 2118.

Place	Date	Hour	Summary of Events and Information	Remarks and references to Appendices
In the Field	25/10/18		Railhead Pt J.S.E. then by L.R. to Braucourt. One lorry to Railhead 6 tons horseshoes and trench clothing. Collected 168 lbs of soft soap & 168 lbs grease also from no IX CT no 2.	
	26/10/18		Visited 14 Bde HQrs, 97 Bde HQrs, 10 A & S Hrs. Bordeaux and R 4/4/1. No truck, Sent lorry to OO IV AT no 1 to collect 16 packsaddles. Sent lorry to OO IX CT no 2 and collected 80 gls oil (nut), 336 grease lub. and 672 lbs soap soft as none is coming from Base. Visited Details, Royal Scots & 15 H + I and 14 T.M.B.	
	27/10/18		Issue R of drawers & coats sheepskin knits. Visited CRA. A,B, & D Btics 161. HQ Co 1, 9 2 sections DAC.	
	28/10/18		Visited Salvage Dump. 2 truck 6-verys units c/o 91 of oil & grease arrived at Railhead and were transferred to light railway. Inspected by H100 IX Corps	
	29/10/18 30/10/18		Cleared stores from Demuille railhead. S. Visited 6 Div salvoes as I am taking over his dump. Decided to move tomorrow 31st inst. the lorry to do IV A T no 1 to collect 7 pkg packsaddleny for 16 (Pioneers) H.L.I. & 8 Revolvers. two lorries salvage to Railhead. bre	
	31/10/18		lorry to 96th Bde. Moved to PAUSIG N.J.	

W. Murcheson Maj
DADOS 37 Div

War Diary
of
D.A.D.O.S. 32nd (Brit.) Division

Vol. 3.   No. 11   (November 1918.)

WAR DIARY / INTELLIGENCE SUMMARY

Army Form C. 2118.

Vol 32

Place	Date	Hour	Summary of Events and Information	Remarks and references to Appendices
In the field	1/11/18	-	Lorry sent to clear Railhead - Road - 1500 Lifebelts received -	
" "	2/11/18	-	1 Lorry sent for 50 pts. Packsaddlery from O.T. N° 1. - 5 Lorry loads of Stores - (Regtl Horse - Vets, Drawn collected from Railhead) Major Pritchard granted leave absence 4th to 18th to U.K. 150 Lifebelts & Tent Pins delivered to 14th & 96th Divs. - 104 Aerr Hand & 105 Railheads drawn from 9 Kings 103 Dump.	
" "	3/11/18		Packsaddlery - Aerr Hand & Railheads sent to Hqrs Adv Hqrs for DAC Train. Lorry to work for Stores - 3 Lorry loads of Brown Meats etc to Baths.	
" "	4/11/18		Received 7 Two Sent Stores from Provencort - Obtained 3 Kokkers Suino from HP for the 118th. Also took in a Lorry load of Belongings Washing (Drawers Cotton) from Baths officer.	
" "	5/11/18		Railhead moves to Mixhigny Farm. - Received K.T. Body - Limber & Wagon R.E also 10 Two Horse Shoes etc. - including dont Supply of first Cars - Taps & Wrenches.	
" "	6/11/18		Returned 1300 Lifebelts to OO 9 CT. N° 1 - Collected Stores from J.P. 1 Lorry sent for Rations & 1 Lorry to 32 DAC with Stores.	
" "	7/11/18		Lorry sent with Stores to Div R.A Stores - 9 1 to 16 H.L.I.C. Train. 1 to 14 Pete H.Q. - 2 Lorries of Salvage Blanket Stores returned to Railhead	
" "	8/11/18		Railhead changed to Frévent - Visited "Q" office at Frévent and was instructed to move tomorrow to Brunnel.	
" "	9/11/18		Party moved Dump to Farm. - 10 Lorries of Stores moved. 10 Tons of Tent floors - Lighters etc. received.	

WAR DIARY or INTELLIGENCE SUMMARY

Army Form C. 2118.

Place	Date	Hour	Summary of Events and Information	Remarks and references to Appendices
S.M. Feb	10/11		Moved 7 lorry loads of Stores from Busigny to Fresnoy - and 9 to Avesnes	
-"-	11/11		3 Lorries to Avesnes - no lorries returned.	
-"-	12/11		Moved office to Avesnes - and 4 lorry loads from Fresnel. 1 lorry from Busigny.	
-"-	13/11		6 lorries of Stores from Fresnel - also cleared Ammo. Shops & personnel to Avesnes. Issues of Clothing & Prot. Eqpt. at Co. to various units.	
-"-	14/11		Attended a conference at "Q." - Sent 1 lorry into Tintage to Busigny + Handies on Tintage + Hot food canteen at Busigny - Sent 3 lorry loads of Supplies Stores to Brie. - Further large issues.	
-"-	15/11		4 lorry loads of Surplus stores Salvage to Railhead - Ord. 2 Trio of reserve of things 8 lorry loads of Salvage Kerosine Stoves. Dept. of Railhead which moves to Vaux. Andigny - 1 lorry to Sams de Nord. for meat ration etc	
-"-	16/11		Clothing issued from bk Cafes - also Major Dunker. Major hands "Cam collete" from Mr. Pytham & brought back to Fresnoy. 4 lorry loads of supply stores returning to Railhead. - 5 how West returned to their Unit - also 2 men who were on short course of instruction Steno. Pays O.M.M.P.D. 8.6.5 am Called and made arrangement regarding staying Point Personnel	
-"-	17/11		7 lorries 1 Ordce Stores to Railhead - also moves sent to Office and Staff to Molain & 1000 Blankets from O.O. 4 Army 7. N° 1 Card 3700 4 from N° 2 A.T. Card delivered to Battalions	

WAR DIARY or INTELLIGENCE SUMMARY

Army Form C. 2118.

(Erase heading not required.)

Place	Date	Hour	Summary of Events and Information	Remarks and references to Appendices
In the Field	19/11	20.00	Took balance of Office Stores to Mulans with 2 horses - also visited Railhead in connection with Office Stores for Brit. Offr. I brought with me one Stock Shed & Bgrt. Offr. & in charge of same Stmn. Barnett. Sent to Bri. Hospital Tailor Shoemaker Saddler & Storeman. Left Pte. Walker at Avenas - at Sleeping place.	
"	20/11		Arranged with R.T.O. to leave L/Cpl. Betts & L/Cpl. Ahmuck at Railhead to check in consignment of Ord. Stores to Corps lorries. General cleaning up & rearranging kits etc. Drew 3 days Rations, 7 Tins Horse Shoes & 3 Trucks Blankets & Nails. Also Waymh H. Sfo Boots & K.T. 2/Amp.L. Major Burchas carried of Crowe attrd. Wells.	
	21/11		Visited 96/5 Bde, 15 Lancs 97th Bde 10 Aq 5 H.q. 104 H.L. 4th Bde, R.E. Donato 15th 4tr 9 H.qs R.A. Firms most units very short of horseshoes prepared for first cargo. Visited A.D.O.T.Y. Corps.	
	22/11		Sent to Railhead (80 kilometres) and found office & staff. Two Arrangements unsatisfactory as B.M.Co. quite not of touch with units. Them 6 00 IX OT to draw for nails authorised on his A.W. 886 d/y 14/18 and found key had none. Meanwhile 70 boxes of Shoes horse & mule - topped - had arrived at Oudetto. Sent the W.O. away busy all day issuing. 3600 Blankets also arrived.	
	23/11		Asked D.w. for lorry to move office & Bde offrs from Railhead. Run unable to supplied. Wrote & told BMOoto to come at by Infty. lorries.	

Army Form C. 2118.

WAR DIARY
or
INTELLIGENCE SUMMARY

(Erase heading not required.)

Instructions regarding War Diaries and Intelligence Summaries are contained in F. S. Regs., Part II. and the Staff Manual respectively. Title Pages will be prepared in manuscript.

Place	Date	Hour	Summary of Events and Information	Remarks and references to Appendices
	25.11.18		Sent for 115 boxes of horseshoes & onto shoes arrived, and 800 pairs of Boots during the day.	
	26.11.18		Sent party 15 D IN A.M. to collect 70 horses horse shoes & some foot nails from OC IV Corps Office. BWCS arrived during the evening.	
	27.11.18		Stayed in Office.	
	28.11.18		Moved RH Quarters. Went there and fixed billet 35 Rue Landrecies for Business staff. Worked till 3 — 15 o'clock no tram arrived.	
	29.11.18		Came with X Coys at 2359 actual R. Remained in Office.	
	30.11.18		No stores arrived. Ordered Lieut "B" to obtain 2 days divisional orders on red no stores arrived. 30th	

War Diary
of
D.A.D.O.S. 32nd Div.

December 1918
Vol. 3 - No. 12

D.A.D.O.S. 32nd DIVISION (stamp)

WAR DIARY or INTELLIGENCE SUMMARY

Army Form C. 2118.

Place	Date	Hour	Summary of Events and Information	Remarks and references to Appendices
M.T.R.D.	1/12/18		No stores arrived.	
	2/12/18		5 lorry load of Breeches received	
	3/12/18		Railhead moved to KANDREGIES. One lorry load of stores was sent out to 5 lorry loads of petrol, paint, soap, oil, grease, lubricating gear & wheels arrived from lorry head. One load of clothing also. Sorry head Kandrigies	
	4/12/18		One load to 114th Bde. Scanter	
	5/12/18		One load to 114th Bde. One load to 16 SBn R.F.A. Sent to 115th Bde. One load had not arrived. 2 loads returned & loads sent back found may of precautions. Went to lorry head. Went to find RofRu (R. Roger) had conflict. Took me over to lorry head. Saw one a fw ldgs. One Rindies to be DIAPh. have staff from railhead to form one a few ldgs. One Rindies would be Kandrieiro Staff from railhead arrived. Informes Rauthead on 11th 8th but that no stores would arrive till 9th.	
	7/12/18		Took representative to Rauthead & found truck had arrived from stand	
	8/12/18		Visited 32nd Bn M.G.C.	
	9/12/18			
	10/12/18		Went to Brussels & ordered 400 Kilos from Service column by order of "Q" Office.	

WAR DIARY or INTELLIGENCE SUMMARY

Army Form C. 2118.

Place	Date	Hour	Summary of Events and Information	Remarks and references to Appendices
A.D.Div	11.12.18		Sent W.O. to DINANT to find billets.	
	12.12.18		Railhead DINANT. First lorry loads of boots arrived at A.D.P.	
	13.12.18		Sent 4 lorries back to A.D.P. to bring up boots. 15% allowed by D.H.Q. A172/18/B1 of 24.11.18 included in the load.	
	14.12.18		One lorry to Bonsecours to collect paint ordered W6218 one lorry to 14th Bde. One lorry to Bonsecours with paint.	
	15.12.18		Lorries to 96, 97 & Artillery. Lorry returned from Bonsecours.	
	16.12.18		Railhead moved to CINEY. Went to find store in Rotoye as Ciney is out of our area. No suitable site. 14 lorries arrived from Base (Horseshoe parts, oil, Austin, grease & oak.) One lorry to 14th Bde.	
	17.12.18		Motor Reserve. Emptying to find new dumps. Found suitable place outside Emptinne but in 66th Division. Asked 66th Div if we could have it. Promised at no R.R.D. early. 2 lorries to Div Artillery. One to 96th Bde., one to 97th Bde. Lorries of 14th Bde came in to draw.	
	18.12.18		No train arrived. Was expecting truck. One lorry to Artillery with 15% overive of boots etc. One to 97th Bn with ditto.	
	19.12.18		One gun for 5 A.F.A. arrived railhead.	
	20.12.18		One French civ. two horseshoes & tube merchants tried to find place for dump near Railhead with dag bag. No suitable site available.	
	21.12.18		131 bales of blankets arrived at railhead. Some distributed, one to 97th Bde. remainder brought in to store.	
	22.12.18		Visited Avenue & found a store. No truck.	

WAR DIARY *or* **INTELLIGENCE SUMMARY**
(Erase heading not required.)

Army Form C. 2118

Place	Date	Hour	Summary of Events and Information	Remarks and references to Appendices
In the field	23/12/18		6 trucks arrived at CINEY. 3 containing Latrine Buckets - 2 blankets & one old Rolph grease paint etc. Trucks had been broken into. Part scattered about. Railhead at Acoese. Hoped to move - but was unable as lorries busy at Ciney.	
	24/12/18		Partly moved to Acoese. 4 trucks arrived at Acoese - unable to offload.	
	25/12/18		Completed move to Acoese.	
	26/12/18		Cleared 7 trucks from railhead S. (3 trucks of latrine buckets than S had accompanied from Ciney) one of clothing, 3 of wagon parts etc & and oxygen stores. 1 truck of clothing had been broken into. Issued to 1/5 Bde, 2 Artillery & R10 Reception Camp. Received 8 lorry loads of French Covers from Div Std Q.C. for despatch to Base.	
	27/12/18			
	28/12/18		Truck of horseshoes one lorry to 14th Bde, one lorry to Reception Camp. Party loaded French Covers. Many units came in to draw.	
	29/12/18		No truck. Units drawing from dump.	
	30/12/18		Two trucks arrived. One of oil, shovels etc, other oil grease etc. Many units drawing.	
	31/12/18		No truck R. One lorry to 14 & 16 Bde. one to Reception Camp, one to 97th Bde.	

Lieut [signature]
ADOS 32 Div

www.ingramcontent.com/pod-product-compliance
Lightning Source LLC
Chambersburg PA
CBHW081401160426
43193CB00013B/2079